OUR BEST FRIENDS

Ferrets

Our Best Friends

OUR BEST FRIENDS

Ferrets

Holly J. Sullivant, DVM

ELDORADO INK

Produced by OTTN Publishing, Stockton, New Jersey

Eldorado Ink
PO Box 100097
Pittsburgh, PA 15233
www.eldoradoink.com

First printing

1 3 5 7 9 8 6 4 2

Library of Congress Cataloging-in-Publication Data

Sullivant, Holly J.
  Ferrets / Holly J. Sullivant.
      p. cm. — (Our best friends)
  Includes index.
  ISBN 978-1-932904-27-7 (hardcover) — ISBN 978-1-932904-35-2 (trade edition)
  1. Ferrets as pets—Juvenile literature. I. Title.
  SF459.F47S85 2008
  636.976'628—dc22
                              2008033057

Photo credits: Courtesy Association of Exotic Mammal Veterinarians, 73; Courtesy
Erlendaakre, 76; © iStockphoto.com/Leslie Banks, 94, 100; © iStockphoto.com/Juergen Bosse,
3, 26, 39, 56, 61, cover middle inset; © iStockphoto.com/Julie Deshaies, 8; © iStockphoto.com/
Fülöp Gergely, 13; © iStockphoto.com/Verity Johnson, 82; © iStockphoto.com/Jim Jurica, 17,
31; © iStockphoto.com/Ian McDonnell, 43; © iStockphoto.com/Tuyen Nguyen, 40;
© iStockphoto.com/Mehmet Salih, 55; © iStockphoto.com/Vicki Stephenson, 69; Joel Mills, 35;
Courtesy Paddy Patterson/www.flickr.com/photos/mrpattersonsir, 32; Courtesy Pet Sitters
International, 89; Used under license from Shutterstock, Inc., 10, 19, 21, 23, 25, 29, 33, 38,
47, 50, 52, 62, 65, 67, 72, 79, 86, 87, 88, 91, 95, 96, 98, 103, fun fact icon (throughout), cover
images (main, top inset, bottom inset, and back); Courtesy Lindsey Turner, 45, 59.

TABLE OF CONTENTS

Introduction

GARY KORSGAARD, DVM

The mutually beneficial relationship between humans and animals began long before the dawn of recorded history. Archaeologists believe that humans began to capture and tame wild goats, sheep, and pigs more than 9,000 years ago. These animals were then bred for specific purposes, such as providing humans with a reliable source of food or providing furs and hides that could be used for clothing or the construction of dwellings.

Other animals had been sought for companionship and assistance even earlier. The dog, believed to be the first animal domesticated, began living and working with Stone Age humans in Europe more than 14,000 years ago. Some archaeologists believe that wild dogs and humans were drawn together because both hunted the same prey. By taming and training dogs, humans became more effective hunters. Dogs, meanwhile, enjoyed the social contact with humans and benefited from greater access to food and warm shelter. Dogs soon became beloved pets as well as trusted workers. This can be seen from the many artifacts depicting dogs that have been found at ancient sites in Asia, Europe, North America, and the Middle East.

The earliest domestic cats appeared in the Middle East about 5,000 years ago. Small wild cats were probably first attracted to human settlements because plenty of rodents could be found wherever harvested grain was stored. Cats played a useful role in hunting and killing these pests, and it is likely that grateful humans rewarded them for this assistance. Over time, these small cats gave up some of their aggressive wild behaviors and began living among humans. Cats eventually became so popular in ancient Egypt that they were believed to possess magical powers. Cat statues were placed outside homes to ward off evil spirits, and mummified cats were included in royal tombs to accompany their owners into the afterlife.

Today, few people believe that cats have supernatural powers, but most pet owners feel a magical bond with their pets, whether they are dogs, cats, hamsters, rabbits, horses, or parrots. The lives of pets and their people become inextricably intertwined, providing strong emotional and physical rewards for both humans and animals. People of all ages can benefit from the loving companionship of a pet. Not surprisingly, then, pet ownership is widespread. Recent statistics indicate that about 60 percent of all households in the United States and Canada have at least one pet, while the figure is close to 50 percent of households in the United Kingdom. For millions of people, therefore, pets truly have become their "best friends."

Finding the best animal friend can be a challenge, however. Not only are there many types of domesticated pets, but each has specific needs, characteristics, and personality traits. Even within a category of pets, such as dogs, different breeds will flourish in different surroundings and with different treatment. For example, a German Shepherd may not be the right pet for a person living in a cramped urban apartment; that person might be better off caring for a smaller dog like a Toy Poodle or Shih Tzu, or perhaps a cat. On the other hand, an active person who loves the outdoors may prefer the companionship of a Labrador Retriever to that of a small dog or a passive indoor pet like a goldfish or hamster.

The joys of pet ownership come with certain responsibilities. Bringing a pet into your home and your neighborhood obligates you to care for and train the pet properly. For example, a dog must be housebroken, taught to obey your commands, and trained to behave appropriately when he encounters other people or animals. Owners must also be mindful of their pet's particular nutritional and medical needs.

The purpose of the OUR BEST FRIENDS series is to provide a helpful and comprehensive introduction to pet ownership. Each book contains the basic information a prospective pet owner needs in order to choose the right pet for his or her situation and to care for that pet throughout the pet's lifetime. Training, socialization, proper nutrition, potential medical issues, and the legal responsibilities of pet ownership are thoroughly explained and discussed, and an abundance of expert tips and suggestions are offered. Whether it is a hamster, corn snake, guinea pig, or Labrador Retriever, the books in the OUR BEST FRIENDS series provide everything the reader needs to know about how to have a happy, well-adjusted, and well-behaved pet.

CHAPTER ONE

Is a Ferret Right for You?

Small sleek bodies, bright button eyes, and adorable whiskered faces—these are the characteristics of the average ferret. Of course, if size were directly correlated with how much trouble an animal could get into, a ferret would be roughly the size of an elephant. Fortunately for them, ferrets are smaller, cuter, and more charming than the average pachyderm wandering the African savannah.

A ferret is a complex bundle of trouble and fun with a keen mind and a mischievous nature. These creatures are small, compact, and agile. Talk to ferret owners and they just might say that ferrets make the perfect pet. Unfortunately, many people are initially taken in by the ferret's beguiling nature and fuzzy appearance only to get in over their heads. Indeed, ferrets are charming creatures, but their care and upkeep require a great deal of work.

The best way to determine if a ferret is the right pet for you is to learn as much as possible about them before committing to ownership. The average ferret lives between five and eight years, with some living to be as old as eleven or twelve, and during that time they depend entirely on their owners for companionship, exercise, and stimulation. As opposed to some pets that need little care other than seeing to their basic needs, ferrets require daily doses of exercise, love, and attention. They also need to be closely supervised while out of their cage, as their fun-loving nature invariably can lead them into trouble.

APPEARANCE AND CHARACTERISTICS

Ferrets are weasels, and, like most members of the weasel family, they have certain distinct traits, including a playful nature and a strong, characteristic scent. Other species of weasels include otters, polecats, badgers, wolverines, minks, and martens. Skunks were once thought to belong to this family, but have been found to be genetically distinct from weasels, despite having a prominent scent gland.

All weasels, including ferrets, are obligate carnivores, or meat eaters. This means they must eat meat exclusively to survive. In the wild, weasels typically live in dens dug into the ground, called burrows.

The European polecat, pictured here, is closely related to the ferret. Ferrets that have escaped or been released into the wild have been known to cross-breed with polecats.

They have sharp claws for digging and are experts at hunting small vermin as prey.

Modern ferrets share many traits with their wild cousins. They, too, have claws for digging, as well as sharp, pointed teeth for tearing and biting. Ferrets have a keen sense of smell and a poor sense of sight—most are nearsighted. All ferrets have small, rounded ears that are close to the head and long, thin tails. They are low to the ground, with short legs and long noses for burrowing and thin, agile bodies that enable them to get out of the tightest holes and the narrowest spaces.

Ferrets sleep a great deal, sometimes as much as eighteen hours a day. The average ferret spends only about 20 to 25 percent of its day playing, eating, and exploring, which is a whole lot to pack into such a short time. Of course, they play so hard that they probably need the other 75 to 80 percent of their lives to rest. Certainly, many people wouldn't object to that arrangement!

On average, male ferrets, or hobs, are larger than their female counterparts, measuring as long as eighteen inches (46 cm) and weighing between two and a half and four pounds (1.1–1.8 kg). Females, referred to as jills, can weigh from as little as a pound (.5 kg) to about three pounds (1.4 kg). Ferrets come in a variety of colors, from a rich sable brown to pure white, with varying patterns.

All ferrets are typically playful, curious, and mischievous creatures that love to explore their surroundings. They are also crepuscular, or most active during the twilight hours of dusk and dawn, something to take into consideration when choosing them as a pet.

FERRET: PERFECT FIT OR NOT?

A ferret is not for everyone. While ferrets themselves are small and seemingly don't take up a lot of room, they somehow manage to quickly fill a household with both personality and paraphernalia. A large cage, toys, food, and bedding all quickly stack up and require at least a small portion of the home

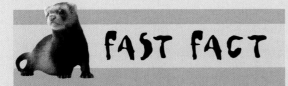

FAST FACT

The black-footed ferret is a wild cousin of the domestic ferret. Black-footed ferrets primarily hunt prairie dogs and were added to the Endangered Species List in 2005. Shrinking habitats and prey levels have led to their decline, and biologists are trying to increase their numbers through conservation efforts.

that is strictly "ferret land." This should typically be in a central area of the home, where the ferrets are in close contact with their human family to get the socialization they need.

The characteristic musky odor of the ferret is very distinctive. This can sometimes be a problem, because the strong odor can permeate most parts of the home. Keeping bedding clean and laundered helps to decrease this scent. Many owners don't mind the scent at all, but it can take some getting used to. This trademark scent is just one example of how ferrets are different from typical house pets.

SOCIAL NATURE: Ferrets are highly social creatures that require a great deal of love and companionship. Average ferrets should spend at least two to four hours a day outside their cage in order to explore, play, and

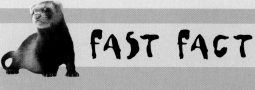

FAST FACT

Ferrets enjoy the company of other ferrets, can often get along quite well with cats, and can eventually coexist peacefully (with care and hard work) with certain breeds of dogs. There have even been ferrets known to live with pet skunks and other "exotic" pets. If a dog and a ferret don't seem to get along, keep them separated. It's better to be safe than sorry.

socialize in the company of their owners. A person who works late hours or has many time commitments might think twice about acquiring a ferret as a pet. While not as time-consuming as most dogs, in terms of walks and interaction, the ferret is by no means a low-maintenance pet that is tucked into a cage to be looked at and then forgotten. Ferrets are actually a lot of work, and ferrets that don't bond with their owners through daily social interaction can become stressed and even ill.

A social ferret is a happy ferret, and while ferrets bond very strongly with their owners, they are also extremely active and sometimes excitable pets. An elderly person might not be an ideal owner, nor would a small child. While children and ferrets would seem to be a perfect fit, ferrets are fairly small critters

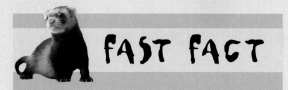

FAST FACT

Ferret aficionados give their beloved friends a wide variety of nicknames, including fuzzies, weasels, furballs, and furries. Male ferrets are officially known as hobs, female ferrets are called jills, and a group of ferrets is referred to as a business.

that resist and sometimes resent the overzealous prodding and high-pitched shrieks of younger children. Young children have been known to drop, throw, or squeeze a ferret to its death. Ferrets are best suited to the quieter, nurturing nature of children over the age of six or seven, who can be taught how to properly interact with and handle them. In any case, ferrets shouldn't be left alone with children, regardless of their age, without adult supervision and, like any other pet, never, ever, with infants.

HUNTING INSTINCT: In choosing a ferret as a pet, another consideration is what other types of animals currently reside in a household. Domestic ferrets were bred for hunting small rodents and vermin, a trait that still characterizes them today. A family that raises hamsters or has a pet parakeet might find themselves in possession of one satisfied ferret and an empty cage, despite the best of precautions.

While horrifying to consider, a ferret's natural inclination is to hunt. For more than two thousand years, people have utilized ferrets precisely for this trait, raising them to "ferret" out or hunt rabbits, rats, and other pests. At the very least, they will play roughly with and quite likely kill pet reptiles, birds, mice, hamsters, and other small

animals. By the same token, a home where terriers or beagles are in residence should also consider the ferret a poor choice. Hunters bred these dogs to hunt small, fuzzy, fast-moving

Ferrets are natural hunters, and will instinctively dig while tracking or chasing prey.

animals—exactly like ferrets. Protecting the ferret might prove both difficult and hair-raising on a daily basis, not to mention the constant whining outside the ferret's cage from a canine pal that feels he's being denied a tasty treat.

TROUBLEMAKING: Let's face it. Trouble never looked quite as adorable as it does on the face of a ferret. Those curious noses and masked faces are completely endearing. They also are the marks of an animal that can and will get into everything. Ferrets are trouble with a capital T.

Ferrets can and will explore holes, cupboards, dresser drawers, and anywhere else they can fit. They have been known to chew and escape through dryer vents. Fabrics and carpets are favorites to gnaw on and dig into. Ferrets also like to hide, often in dangerous places like sofa cushions or behind refrigerators. While ferrets are almost always able to be litter box trained, they also see nothing wrong with using the closest available corner as a toilet if they are playing and too busy to bother finding their litter pan.

They also are natural little thieves (translated loosely, their Latin name,

KEEP AN EYE ON YOUR FERRET

Ferrets are social, playful creatures. When eighteen hours a day are spent asleep, the remaining six need to be as jam-packed as possible with fun and games. All ferrets must be out of their cage for a minimum of two to four hours a day, a serious time commitment. Fortunately, finding ways to entertain a ferret isn't difficult. Generally they'll entertain themselves with just about anything—the remote control, balls, empty toilet paper tubes—which is why it is important to supervise them at all times while they are out and about.

It only takes a ferret a few moments to get into trouble—trouble that can have serious consequences. For example, one of the leading causes of major illness in young ferrets is intestinal blockage. Ferrets love to eat all sorts of strange things when their owners aren't paying attention, and, each year, thousands of pet ferrets end up having emergency surgery to remove foam pieces, strings, buttons, and other unusual objects from their stomachs. When choosing a ferret as a pet, be aware of how much supervision and care one needs, and that ferret ownership is a serious responsibility.

Mustela putorius furo, means "stinky thief") and will make off with anything that captures their interest. Ferret owners often find little nests of socks, jewelry, toys, television remotes, credit cards, and other interesting objects. Most owners quickly learn the location of these hiding places and will check there first when something important goes missing.

Owning a ferret requires constant vigilance and bucketfuls of patience. While the rewards of ferret ownership more than repay this in some people's minds, for others it is just too much. Ferret owners must have a watchful eye and need to completely secure their home from their curious critter.

THE UNSEEN COSTS OF FERRET OWNERSHIP: When buying a ferret, the major expenses are the pet himself, along with his cage, food, toys, litter pans, bedding, and other items. However, there are other costs you must consider before purchasing a ferret. First, of course, is the commitment of your time each day, as ferrets require their owners' love and companionship to thrive. Ferret owners must also be prepared to pay for veterinary care, preventative medications, and stimulating toys for their pets.

If you have to leave on vacation, you will doubtless incur some pet care costs. Boarding facilities are often expensive and many won't admit ferrets. Owners may have to pay a professional sitter if they don't have friends or family members willing to care for their pets.

As with any other animal, before committing to ownership, prospective ferret owners need to closely examine their resources and make an informed decision about whether they can realistically care for a pet. Shelters are full of animals, including ferrets, that well-meaning owners fell in love with and then were unable to care for.

FERRETS AND THE LAW: Another consideration before buying a ferret is if having one is even an option. In certain parts of the world, including in the United States, particular municipalities and states have outlawed ferret ownership.

While many people own ferrets in areas where they are against the law,

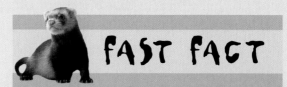

FAST FACT

Ferrets are prohibited in many parts of the country, including particular states, cities, and municipalities. Many military bases also prohibit ferrets. Check local laws before taking a ferret home.

THE COST OF FERRET OWNERSHIP

During an average year, you will spend several hundred dollars on your ferret between the costs of food and medical care. A ferret doesn't eat much, but good-quality ferret food is often costly. Veterinary visits, including an annual checkup with vaccines and blood tests, can amount to several hundred dollars, and monthly flea and heartworm control can also add up. Health insurance is available, but that is also another expense, and you'll want to see what diseases and conditions are covered before you buy it.

At some point in their lives, most ferrets will develop a serious illness that will require additional medical care and expense. While you are considering ferret ownership, make up a budget with monthly and yearly expenses and see if it is workable. It is always a good idea to have a little fund set aside in case of a medical emergency (some veterinarians recommend as much as $500).

this is a risky proposition. Local authorities are within their rights to seize and euthanize illegal ferrets. It is never a good idea to own a ferret if doing so is against the law.

Before purchasing a ferret, find out about local and state laws. Even if ferrets are legal, you may still need to obtain a special permit or license for them. At the minimum, most areas require ferrets to have proof of rabies vaccination and a county license. (See Chapter 3 for more information on ferret bans.)

THE PERFECT FIT

After all is considered, the ferret is the right pet for a certain type of person. There are cat people and dog people; it would follow suit that there are also ferret people. People who consider all the options, educate themselves, and are willing to commit to providing a safe and loving home for these little "fuzzies," as some call them, may find that a ferret is the perfect fit.

Have a warm heart, infinite patience, the ability to detect a ferret in a couch cushion at ten feet, and the capacity for laughter and fun? Then a ferret might be the perfect fit for you.

CHAPTER TWO

Selecting Your One-of-a-Kind Ferret (or Two)

The relationship between ferrets and people extends back at least two thousand years. There are mentions of ferrets in the writings of the ancient Romans and pictures of ferret-like creatures have been found among the tombs of the Egyptians. The origins of the domestic ferret are shrouded in mystery, but it is almost certain that they share ancestry with the European and Steppe polecats—members of the weasel family that are larger than ferrets and that can be successfully bred with them to produce offspring. Whatever their true origin, history shows ferrets firmly ensconced in Western

Spend time with a potential pet ferret to determine whether his personality matches yours.

Europe, primarily the British Isles, sometime around A.D. 600.

Although occasionally known as a companion animal, the ferret's primary role in the past was as a hunter. The ferret was part of a well-oiled hunting machine, and for hundreds of years, teams of men, ferrets, and hunting dogs kept farms and other areas free of pests. Ferrets would be released by their handlers into an area, where they would dig down into the earth and flush out rabbits, plus rats or other vermin, from their hiding places. Dogs, particularly terriers, would then be used to dispatch the creatures.

Cats eventually replaced ferrets as the ratters of choice in many places, due to their agreeable nature and lack of a strong scent, but in many rural areas, ferrets were widely used. Their use as hunters continued through more modern history, and they accompanied Europeans to North America, New Zealand, and Australia. Eventually, with the advent of modern methods of pest control, their use declined and in many places, became illegal. As ferrets fell out of favor as hunters, they took on a new role as laboratory animals and then, later, in the 1960s, evolved into companion animals.

In the past few decades, ferrets exploded in popularity. Today, there are an estimated 2 million ferrets in the United States, making them the country's third most popular pet. This rise in popularity is responsible for the increasing variety and diversity of the ferret population. Once the

FERRETS IN ART

Throughout history, ferrets have been the subject of works of art and even royal patronage. Ferrets were popular pets with royalty, especially white ferrets, which were easily spotted while hunting. White ferrets looked like ermines but were likely much more manageable. Several famous paintings feature ferrets, including "The Ermine Portrait of Queen Elizabeth," by Nicholas Hilliard, which can be seen at Hatfield House, the childhood home of Elizabeth I, outside of London. The ermine in Leonardo da Vinci's famous "Lady with an Ermine" was more likely a white ferret. This painting is currently housed at the Czartoryski Museum in Krakow, Poland. Other works featuring ferrets include tapestries, frescos, and illustrations.

decision has been made to add a ferret to the family, there are many different options to consider.

ONE FERRET OR TWO?

Nothing is as much fun as a ferret, except, perhaps, owning more than one. Many ferret owners swear that having two (and sometimes more) as pets is not only more enjoyable, but also more practical.

While owning two ferrets sounds like quite a bit of work and expense, if you can afford it, it is a wonderful idea. Ferrets are highly social animals, and having a companion to play and snuggle with can go a long way toward enhancing their mental and physical health. While an owner can provide much of the interaction a ferret requires, having another of their kind around to play with makes things that much better. Of course, double the ferrets can also get into double the trouble—two ferrets being even more mischievous than one. But ferrets that are happy and

have a ready and willing playmate may make up for any additional trouble they may get into or messes they might make. Having more than one ferret shouldn't, however, be considered a substitute for the companionship that an owner can and should supply, or an excuse to decrease playtime out of the animal's cage.

A BOY OR A GIRL?

The first thing most people try to decide is whether to get a male or a female. For some people this is a serious consideration, but for the most part, there are few differences in personality between the sexes. Ask any gathering of ferret owners which sex is more cuddly and affectionate or

Ferrets are social creatures by nature. If you can handle two, they will probably appreciate having a playmate.

which roughhouses more during play. There will be a great many different opinions, with some in favor of one or the other.

In general, all ferrets are playful and inquisitive. Some ferrets like cuddling and others are a bit more standoffish. Some may be a bit fearful of strangers and others might gallop up to a visiting guest and say hello. Hobs are larger than their female counterparts, but beyond that, any differences have to do with each ferret's unique personality.

When choosing a ferret, it is better to gauge if its personality is a good fit rather than being set on one particular sex. A jill might be a raucous troublemaker, and the quiet hob in the corner might be the perfect cuddly companion.

A FERRET OF A DIFFERENT COLOR?

Ferrets are found in a wide variety of colors and patterns. Most ferrets have dark brown or black eyes, with the exception of some albino ferrets that have pink or red eyes. Ferrets come in such a wide assortment of colors that even the most particular ferret connoisseur can find one that appeals to her specific taste.

Traditionally, the most common ferret colors have been sable and albino. Sable is a rich dark brown that blends into cream around the mask and face. All ferrets have two

MORE TO LOVE

Sometimes one ferret just isn't enough. Although many people get one ferret first and then later acquire a second one, it is often best to bring more than one ferret home right from the beginning. Kits that have been raised together are usually closely bonded, particularly if they spend a lot of time together in their cage. By the same token, adult rescue ferrets will often have a particular buddy in their shelter or foster home. Ferrets that already get along can spare you a lot of hassle, including battles for dominance.

Even worse, you might find that your newcomer and the previously adopted ferret just won't get along at all.

Having two ferrets is not that much more of a day-to-day expense than keeping one. They can share cage space, litter boxes, and food. The main expense that comes from having more than one ferret is the higher cost of veterinary care. It is important to make sure that each of your ferrets gets the preventative care it requires, and that there is room in the budget for emergencies.

layers of fur. The guard hairs, or the slightly coarse, overlying hairs that provide the protective, greasy outer layer, are dark brown in the sable ferret. Beneath is the softer, fluffier undercoat, which provides insulation and warmth. In the sable, this under-coat is typically cream or white.

Albino ferrets are just what they sound like—cream-colored or white-colored with a slightly lighter under-coat. True albinos possess a recessive genetic trait and have pink or red eyes. White ferrets can also have black or crimson eyes; these are con-sidered dark-eyed whites, rather than true albinos. These ferrets will often have a few darker-colored hairs scat-tered here and there throughout the coat as opposed to the albino's pure white.

Beyond sable and albino, there is a wide range of shades that have been more recently bred, including choco-late, black, cinnamon, and cham-pagne. All are varying degrees of brown, brownish red, or golden cream with lighter undercoats. Ferrets can

Pictured below are two of the most popular ferret colors: white (albino) and sable.

also have a silvery-gray coat, often called pewter or sterling. Varying patterns of these colors exist, including blazes (dark with white feet and white patterns going up onto the chest and head), spots, parti-colored markings (with a white head like a panda), and points—markings similar to those of Siamese cats.

Naturally, all colors and patterns are a matter of personal preference, but blaze and panda ferrets should be considered carefully before being chosen. These color patterns are associated with a disease known as Waardenburg syndrome, which can cause deafness and other health problems.

Interestingly, a ferret's coat color can change throughout its lifetime. Most ferrets will undergo seasonal changes of color from summer to winter, and kits (or baby ferrets) will often change their coat color as

they mature. Kits are also born without the traditional mask, which develops in time. Owners shouldn't be surprised if a young ferret doesn't look quite like a typical ferret should.

No matter what the color, the important thing is that a ferret has a congenial personality and is healthy. Color, after all, is only fur deep.

A HAPPY, HEALTHY FERRET

Once you decide to acquire a pet ferret, the choices can be overwhelming. Color, age, and gender are all irrelevant, however, if you find yourself taking on a ferret with personality problems or health concerns. Foremost in your mind should be the ferret's health and personality.

Ferrets sleep the majority of the day. When choosing a ferret, make several visits at different times of the day to fully assess its personality. A ferret that is cuddly and quiet in the morning might be a rambunctious and unrepentant delinquent later in the day.

All ferrets should have natural curiosity and a playful nature. Inherent differences in sociability will occur from ferret to ferret, but a ferret that acts depressed and shows no interest in toys or its surroundings might be ill and would probably be a poor choice.

FAST FACT

All ferrets being kept as pets should be spayed or neutered. Male ferrets that are neutered are technically referred to as gibs; however, most people continue to refer to them as hobs. Likewise, spayed jills are technically known as sprites, a charming term that is little used.

When choosing a ferret, look him over very carefully. He should be energetic and lively, with clear eyes, ears and nose.

Most people can learn to tell the difference between a healthy ferret and a sick one. The ferret's eyes should be clear and bright, its coat smooth and even, and it should not appear extraordinarily thin and bony. Check for discharge from the nose or evidence of it on the feet, and examine the feet and tail for traces of loose stools. Any ferret that appears sick should not be purchased or adopted, as often these animals are chronically ill and if you took it home, you might incur significant veterinary expenses. When assessing a ferret's overall health, keep in mind that the best person to do this is a qualified veterinarian. Within days of taking your ferret home, it should have a thorough veterinary checkup.

In addition to examining the ferret, scrutinize its environment. At a breeder, ferrets should be kept in large cages with lots of opportunity for social interaction. Single ferrets in small cages may not be properly socialized. At a pet store, a ferret housed in a glass enclosure with cedar shavings, surrounded by birds, and constantly poked at by passersby could have personality or health issues resulting from stress.

A ferret should always be kept in impeccable surroundings, with clean water, good food, and no excessive waste accumulating in corners or litter boxes. Ferrets prefer cozy blankets and snuggly sacks. If your pet store displays a ferret exactly like the hamster beside it, complete with plastic house, shavings, and pieces of carrot, that generally means the store staff are unaware of how ferrets should be housed and fed. Examine such improperly kept ferrets carefully, and take any pet care advice given by the staff with a healthy degree of skepticism. While many pet store employees are educated animal lovers with a great deal of knowledge to share, there are also no requirements to work in a pet store. It is always best to get tips on care and maintenance from a veterinarian or another reputable source.

If feces are present in the cage, examine them to check their consistency. Ferret stool should resemble those of a cat—formed, relatively small, and dark brown in color. Soft or liquid stools should be suspect, and anything greenish or bloody-

looking in color should trigger an alarm that the ferrets in that cage are unhealthy. Even if a particular ferret looks healthy, if it is being kept in a facility with sick ferrets, they may all have been exposed to disease. Look at all the cages and all the ferrets and draw conclusions about the overall health of the group as well as the individuals.

Once it is clear that the ferrets and their environment are healthy, the next step is to interact with all the ferrets. See which are friendlier, which are cuddliest, and which are the most standoffish. Often, it quickly becomes apparent which ferret will suit a prospective owner, but remember that ferret ownership is a long-term commitment and you should not rush into it. Take your time in making a decision. If the ferrets in one facility don't seem quite right, it is perfectly all right to move on. Visit several stores or breeders before committing. Making an impulse buy might be all right with a book or a movie, but a ferret is a living creature. Make sure the ferret that comes home with you is the right one.

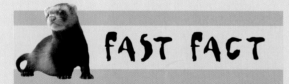

FAST FACT

Blaze and panda ferrets, with their white heads, can be born with a genetic problem that causes deafness. This disease is called Waardenburg syndrome by many ferret experts, because it is similar to a disease of that name that affects people. Deaf ferrets can live as normal a life as any other ferret. They may startle easily, however, and might require special vigilance and care.

TO KIT OR NOT TO KIT?

Another consideration is whether to choose a full-grown ferret or a kit. Kits (baby ferrets) are a bundle of fun. They will bond quite closely with their owners and their new family will have all the joy of bringing up baby. The downside is that kits are babies. They are inquisitive and require a great deal of love and handling to become good ferret citizens. While the average ferret acts like a typical two-year-old, with kits, these traits are magnified.

For some people, an adult ferret that has already earned its stripes might be a better choice. Typically, these ferrets are litter trained and socialized, although they do have some drawbacks. Older ferrets are often obtained through breeders or rescue organizations. They may have been through several owners and could have personality problems or health issues as a result of stress. These ferrets should definitely be checked by a vet, and you should ask lots of questions before taking them home. While older ferrets may be a great choice, it is important first to assess their personality and history to make sure that someone else's problems are not being passed on to you.

What it really comes down to is a matter of common sense. A family with children and a busy lifestyle might be better off choosing an

Although kits are incredibly cute, it is important to remember that raising a baby ferret takes time and patience. A kit might not be the right choice for a first-time ferret owner.

adult ferret that is already litter box trained and prepared for excited hands holding him. Alternatively, a college student with time on her hands might opt for a kit that she can train, bond with, and potentially have for a long time.

Regardless of age, all ferrets should be altered for health reasons. Most are also de-scented, which decreases their odor. In the United States, this is the standard for young ferrets, although in European coun-tries, early spay/neuter of ferrets is rare, and in the United Kingdom, de-scenting is illegal.

WHERE DO FERRETS COME FROM?

To find a ferret, you have to know where to look. For some people, it is as easy as going to the corner pet store. Others, in more rural locales, may have to go a bit farther afield. With a little research, it is easy to find ferrets, both kits and adults, looking for good homes. Breeders,

Ask people you know that own ferrets if they can recommend a local breeder. The Internet can also be used to find a breeder near you. When you visit a ferret breeder, take a close look at the facilities. If the cages and living quarters don't appear clean and well-kept, and the ferrets look dirty or sick, you probably want to avoid purchasing a pet from that breeder.

pet stores, animal rescue leagues, and shelters are all possible sources, each with pros and cons.

BREEDER: For some people, breeders are the only way to go. A breeder is a well-educated layperson with a love for ferrets. Ferret breeding requires immense dedication and skill. Not just anyone can breed ferrets. Ferret breeders are also usually very conscientious. Rarely will you take home a poor-quality animal from a breeder. Still, choosing a breeder should be done with careful consideration. The Internet, local ferret clubs, and ads in ferret publications are all good places to find lists of local breeders.

A breeder should be willing to have her facilities and animals inspected, and she should be open to answering any questions. In fact, you may find that the breeder is interviewing you! Breeders become very attached to their "fuzzies" and want to make sure they are going to good, caring homes. They often have a wide selection of ferrets of differing colors and ages to choose from.

Look for evidence that the breeder's animals are healthy and well-socialized and closely examine the facilities. They should be clean and well-kept. Available ferrets should also be altered and de-scented. If this has

not been done, the purchase price should be much lower than if it is. In either case, expect to spend a fair amount when buying a ferret. The cost of a ferret varies from place to place; most ferrets fall into a $75–$250 price range, and about $125 is typical. Fortunately, this typically includes first vaccinations, altering, and de-scenting, and could be considered something of a bargain. Having a ferret altered at a later time is almost as costly as buying a ferret outright.

Animals from breeders come from a known source, and breeders often encourage follow-up questions and are happy to address your concerns. Usually, they will also offer a health guarantee. This can be invaluable. Unfortunately, ferret breeding is time-consuming and expensive. Small breeders that hand raise their

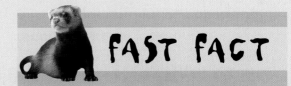

FAST FACT

When purchasing a ferret from a breeder or a pet store, ask about health guarantees. Most states have specific laws about the sale of animals, and many require a health certificate signed by a veterinarian and listing all vaccinations given. In addition, animals may need to be examined by a veterinarian within a short time of purchase for a guarantee to be valid.

kits are hard to find in some areas, and sometimes a drive of several hundred miles is necessary to find a good source.

PET STORES: The mainstay for the average ferret buyer, pet stores are both convenient and accessible. In most areas there is a pet store within a reasonable driving distance that offers ferrets for sale. Unfortunately, the selection at pet stores is often limited to a few ferrets or sometimes only one. It is also difficult to ascertain a ferret's personality in a quick visit during which it is also being poked and prodded by people buying cat litter and hamster treats.

Ferrets in pet stores typically come from either local breeders or one of several large-scale breeding operations in the United States. For the most part, these operations are reputable, and their animals are socialized and have had good veterinary care, including being altered and de-scented. However, their ferrets usually travel a good distance to get to the shop, and may arrive anxious or stressed.

The cost of a ferret in a pet store should typically be about the same as it is at a breeder and include altering, de-scenting, and first vaccinations. Use caution if the price seems unnaturally steep.

Some pet stores will mark up pets as much as several hundred dollars if they are extremely popular. Make sure the price is reasonable and fair and that falling for a ferret doesn't lead to being taken for a ride.

While pet stores are convenient, never purchase a pet store ferret (or any animal, for that matter) on a lark. Ferrets, like any pet, are a huge commitment. Take time to consider available ferrets, ask to hold them and examine them, and be cautious if answers to your questions are evasive or if the ferrets and facilities appear to be subpar. While it is natural to want to take home and "fix" a sickly ferret or one that has been languishing in a pet store, these ferrets often have major problems, which can be both emotionally and financially draining. Let any special needs

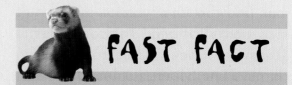

FAST FACT

Animal shelters and rescue organizations all over the country—many devoted exclusively to ferrets—are often in need of foster parents to take ferrets for both long and short periods. Being a foster parent can be a great introduction to ferrets and can sometimes turn into a permanent, lasting relationship.

Shelters and rescue organizations are full of ferrets seeking new homes. Before purchasing from a breeder, why not find out if you can help a ferret in need?

ferrets at pet stores (or breeders and shelters, for that matter) go to people experienced with ferrets, who are willing to assume the commitment they require. First-timers and hobbyists should always put health and personality first.

SHELTERS AND FERRET RESCUE LEAGUES: It stands to reason that if dogs and cats end up in shelters, ferrets would as well. Ferrets are surrendered to shelters for various reasons, from the tragic to the mundane. Some ferrets come from homes that simply could not handle the time commitment they required, while others are taken from places where they suffered from inadequate care or sometimes outright neglect.

A shelter is a good place to find a ferret friend. Many local animal shelters have ferrets up for adoption, mostly adults, but some kits. An Internet search will usually turn up several rescue organizations that are within driving distance. Shelter ferrets are often available for free or for a nominal adoption fee (often up to $50 less than an average store or breeder ferret), and are usually vaccinated, altered, and sometimes even microchipped.

Lower cost doesn't mean adopting a ferret from a shelter is the easy option, however. When adopting from an organization, it is extremely important to find out where the ferret came from and how it happened to come to the shelter. Unfortunately, most rescue organizations know little about the history of the ferrets they care for beyond what is listed on their health records. While owners are usually asked to list the reasons they are giving up their pets, there is no way to determine how truthful those answers are.

A ferret from a rescue organization is an unknown quantity. On the flip side, these ferrets are often placed in temporary foster homes, with caregivers who can offer good insight into their personality and needs. Rescue and shelter ferrets are very special. Adopting an animal that truly needs a loving home is a wonderful experience, providing an owner with both a good feeling and a loving life-long friend.

CHAPTER THREE

Responsible Ferret Ownership

Ferrets are inherently lovable, from their whiskered faces to their endearing personalities. Falling in love with a ferret is easy, but being a responsible pet owner involves more than just feelings of affection. As with any other pet, owning a ferret comes with a list of obligations and responsibilities. Quality food, shelter, companion-ship, exercise, and proper health care will all ensure your ferret a long and happy life. These things come at a price, however, both financially and in time spent.

WHAT DO FERRETS NEED?

Ferrets don't need an enormous cage and expensive toys to keep them happy. Ferrets will be happy with

Ferrets thrive on human contact. Beyond the basic needs, your ferret needs your companionship.

Your ferret will want to be involved with your family on a daily basis. Place his cage in a central area of your home where he can see you. He'll feel like he's interacting even though he's in his cage.

almost any toy as long as it stimulates their natural sense of play and fun. Cages don't have to be mansions as long as they are safe, adequate in size, and have a cozy place to snuggle. Ferrets are just as content in a slightly smaller cage as they are in an enormous penthouse. Still, you shouldn't expect to keep a ferret housed most of the day in a tiny carrier or a dog cage. Special ferret cages are available for purchase. In general, these are escape-proof and are sized and made with ferrets in mind.

No matter what the size, a ferret's cage should be escape-proof and kept in a quiet area that is accessible to the family. A ferret shouldn't be kept next to the washer and dryer or tucked away in a back bedroom. Ferrets need to be somewhere central, where they can participate in household life, even when they're not out playing.

The cage should be kept neat and clean, with laundered blankets or sleep sacks, litter boxes, and clean food and water bowls that are changed daily. Good-quality ferret food that meets the animal's nutritional needs and fresh water should be always available. A variety of toys should also be provided, both in the cage and in the play area. Finally ferrets should be given ample time each day for supervised play outside their cage and social interaction with their family. While some ferrets spend all their time outside their cage exploring and playing, most also take some of this time to cuddle or socialize with their owners. Playtime is a special experience for owner and ferret, deepening the bond they share.

Last, but possibly most important, is regular, professional health

Your ferret doesn't have to have just one cage. If you have the resources, you may want to give your ferret an outdoor cage so that he can be safely outside with you and your family.

care. Yearly veterinary exams and appropriate vaccinations are essential to the health and well-being of all ferrets. Kits or senior ferrets may require more frequent visits for vaccines or wellness checkups. While high-quality care may be somewhat costly, it is more than worth the money to guarantee that your ferret lives a long and happy life.

KEEPING FERRETS HAPPY, HEALTHY, AND SAFE

IDENTIFICATION: Ferrets are smart, curious, and quick. Despite your best efforts at ferret-proofing, mishaps can happen. An opened door or an unlatched cage can lead to a lost pet. Natural disasters, such as hurricanes or tornados, can unexpectedly separate even the most careful and devoted owners from

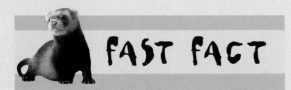

FAST FACT

The time to start looking for a veterinarian is before you bring your ferret home. Most new ferrets should have a checkup in the first few days, so it's best to have a veterinarian already chosen to make the process as seamless as possible. This is especially important if a new ferret gets sick. The first visit to a vet shouldn't be an emergency.

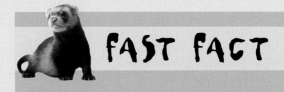

FAST FACT

Ferret shopping list: cage, bedding (sleep sack or hammock), dry ferret food, treats, heavy ceramic food and water bowls and/or a large water bottle, corner-shaped litter boxes (at least three), litter scoop, toys, harness or collar, identification tag, litter.

their pets. An identification tag or a more permanent identification method can mean the difference between a ferret that is forever lost and one that is reunited with its family.

Traditionally, collars with tags have been used to identify pets. While inexpensive and often effective, collars can be lost or deliberately removed. Most ferrets wear breakaway cat collars or harnesses. Breakaway collars, which come apart if caught on something, are easily lost and often unreliable when it comes to providing identification.

Permanent methods of identification, including tattooing and microchipping, are becoming increasingly common. Tattooing is a method long relied on to identify animals. A tattoo is a small identification code or symbol that is placed on the ear or inner thigh when an animal is very young. Unfortunately, tattoos may fade over time. Another problem is that there are also no national databases for ferret tattoos. While tattooing is a good way to identify a particular ferret, it is not the best way to recover a lost or stolen pet.

Microchipping is a reliable, if relatively new, technology. A microchip is a tiny radio transmitter, the size of a grain of rice, that is injected under the skin in between the animal's shoulder blades. Most veterinarians and shelters perform the procedure, and it is safe, affordable, and completed with minimal discomfort to the animal. Shelters and veterinarians have special scanners that pick up the radio waves transmitted by the chip. The chip holds a unique number that

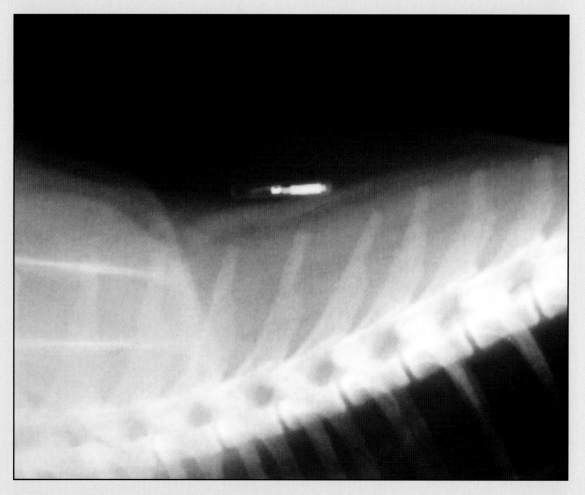

This X-ray shows a microchip (the long, bright spot) implanted in a pet's back. The microchip won't hurt your ferret, but it will make it easier to identify him as yours if he is lost or stolen.

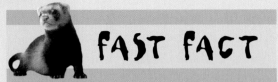

FAST FACT

In recent years, microchips have been surrounded by controversy. The main concern has been that lost pets were not being reunited with their owners because several different types of scanners and chips were in use. Fortunately, this process is becoming streamlined: Universal chips and readers are soon to become standardized by international law.

is registered to the animal in a national database. Microchip identification is a good idea for all ferrets and is also required for travel to certain foreign countries.

SPAYING AND NEUTERING: Like dogs and cats, ferrets make better, healthier pets if they are spayed and neutered. While controlling the pet population is not as important a concern with ferrets as it is with other animals, all pet ferrets should be spayed or neutered for their own well-being. Female ferrets that are not spayed and do not breed will develop a life-threatening medical condition due to constantly being in heat, and ferrets of both sexes typically have a stronger smell.

While many people think about breeding their pet ferrets simply because they would love to be surrounded by adorable baby kits, ferret breeding is a time-consuming and difficult process that is best left to professional breeders rather than hobbyist owners. A person interested in breeding will have difficulty finding intact ferrets to breed, and kits require an enormous amount of socialization and human contact to make them good pets. Many large-scale breeders hire employees to do nothing more than work with the kits. If breeding is an interest of yours, you should keep ferrets for a considerable time before making the decision.

PET INSURANCE: Like human health care, veterinary care doesn't come cheap. Wellness visits and annual vaccines alone can add up, but when a ferret is sick, the cost of diagnosis

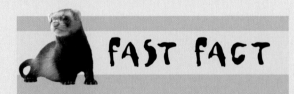

FAST FACT

Most veterinarians can provide information on recommended insurance providers. VPI, which has been providing affordable and reliable veterinary insurance in the United States since 1982 (longer than any other carrier), is considered to be the most widely recommended pet insurance company by veterinarians.

SPAYING AND NEUTERING

For some species of animals, spaying and neutering are both measures to control pet population and recommended for the animal's health. For female ferrets, however, spaying is essential. Jills that are not bred will continually stay in heat and can develop a life-threatening form of anemia. Hobs, on the other hand, can become aggressive if they are not neutered. The odor of intact ferrets is also particularly strong.

In most cases, particularly if they are purchased from a pet shop, ferrets are altered and de-scented at an early age, before they are even shipped from the breeding facility. Many private breeders also will have their baby ferrets (or kits) altered before they are sold. This is included in the purchase price and may be an important consideration when deciding to buy a particular ferret, since having an older ferret spayed or neutered is expensive.

Some research has linked early spaying and neutering to hormonal disease later in life; so in some countries, this procedure is put off until ferrets are six to eight months of age. In the United States, early spaying and neutering is the norm, due to the expense and sometimes the difficulty of doing it later. With increased owner awareness, early spays and neuters may become less common, which could lead to longer ferret life spans.

and treatment can become quite substantial. Since ferrets can't be made to go out and get a job to pay for their health care, pet insurance is a good option to consider.

Pet insurance is available for many kinds of pets, including ferrets, and typically provides for wellness care and vaccines as well as covering various illnesses. Like human medical insurance, there is usually a deductible to be met, after which the insurance reimburses a percentage of all medical costs. Depending on the illness and treatment, insurance can save a pet owner hundreds of dollars. There are few downsides to pet insurance beyond the cost of premiums, as long as the policy is purchased from a legitimate, well-known provider. The main benefit to pet insurance is that it helps insure that pets receive timely and appropriate medical care. In the end, this leads to a happier, healthier pet.

FERRETS RUNNING AFOUL OF THE LAW: While it's difficult to imagine how anyone couldn't love a ferret, there are quite a few places where owning them is actually against the law. Some municipalities and states have passed laws regulating or banning ferrets ownership. In both California and Hawaii, for instance,

Before purchasing a ferret, check with your local animal control official to make sure they are legal in your municipality or state.

it is against the law to possess a ferret. Ferret ownership is illegal in New York City, although ferrets are permitted elsewhere in the state.

Many people own ferrets despite local bans, but there are risks involved when breaking the law. Owners of illegal ferrets may find themselves facing stiff fines. Local authorities can seize and, in some cases, even destroy their pets. There are constant battles between local ferret groups and governments over restrictive ordinances. Dedicated ferret lovers have overturned restrictions in many areas, but in some places changing the law has proven difficult, if not impossible.

Before bringing a ferret home, research local laws and ordinances regarding ferret-keeping. Even if owning a ferret is legal, most municipalities require ferrets to be up-to-date on their rabies vaccine and properly licensed or registered. Some states even require spaying or neutering. It is also wise to check with landlords or home-owner associations before buying a ferret. Some landlords will not rent to owners of ferrets and consider pet ferrets grounds for eviction. Finding out what the laws and rules are ahead of time is always wise and can prevent future heartaches for owners and their furry bandits.

Being a responsible ferret owner is key to ensuring that you and your ferret have a long, happy, and healthy life together.

CHAPTER FOUR

The Best Possible Beginning

Once you decide to bring a ferret into your family, it is important to prepare for the new arrival before it comes home. Engaging in frantic last-minute preparations while a worried and stressed ferret waits in a travel carrier is hardly the best way to welcome a new family member.

Ferrets will come into their new environment a little overwhelmed and anxious, so be sure to have a safe place set up for them to relax

Picking up excess clutter around your home is a key step in ferret-proofing your home. Ferrets are very curious animals and will get into just about everything as they explore their surroundings.

and regroup. It won't take long until all your ferrets feel confident enough to poke their nose out of their cozy sleep sack or hammock and become acquainted with their cage, their toys, and their new family. For their well-being, however, cage, home, and family must be prepared in advance.

PREPARING YOUR HOME AND FAMILY

It is debatable whether a first-time ferret owner is ever prepared for the joys and chaos a new ferret will bring to a home. Like bringing home a new baby or a puppy, you must be aware of how much trouble such a small creature can get into in a short time.

Ferrets are smart, quick, flexible, and naturally curious. They will explore, pilfer, and make themselves at home in no time flat. Sometimes they will get into serious trouble, possibly even danger. Ferrets have a flexible spine that enables them to crawl into incredibly tight spaces, and their innate curiosity will lead them anywhere large enough for their head to fit in. They also have an unnatural appetite for substances such as rubber, foam, and plastic. To cut down on the chaos and to ensure the ferret's safety, ferret-proofing your home is absolutely essential before the ferret even sets paw into the home.

FERRET-PROOFING YOUR HOME:

When ferret-proofing your home, look at everything in the house—low, high, and hidden. There are many unforeseen dangers in homes that most people don't even consider until it is too late. Keep in mind as you're ferret-proofing that ferrets can also be destructive. They like to dig into potted plants and can often destroy furniture or carpeting with their overly enthusiastic burrowing.

From the beginning, decide which rooms your ferret is allowed to access. Keep the rest of the house off limits by closing doors or installing special ferret-proof gates. To a ferret, children's rooms are fascinating as well as dangerous—a source of fun things like silly putty, Nerf balls, and other potentially harmful items. Bathrooms are also full of hazards, including medicines, cleaning products, and trashcans brimming with interesting stuff. Most people make bathrooms and their children's rooms off-limits to ferrets because of the potential dangers and the difficulty of completely ferret-proofing these spaces.

Once a ferret's play area has been determined, secure or stash all electrical cords and wires out of a ferret's reach. Ferrets are especially fond of speaker wires and computer cables. Various devices are available in hardware or electronics stores for this purpose.

Next, scout out all small, appealing objects that are either dangerous or valuable. Ferrets love pens, jewelry, hard candies, shoelaces, children's toys, paper, erasers, socks, paper clips—everything and anything that can easily be picked up and ferreted away. Some things that might not even seem appealing can disappear; just ask a ferret owner who has lost a remote control or a cell phone. Fortunately, most ferrets have a hiding spot under a bed or in a quiet corner of the house. Once this is discovered, it is easier to find a missing treasure, like an expensive watch. Take special care to secure small, sharp objects, such as needles or nails, and items made of rubber or foam, which ferrets love to chew but which can cause intestinal blockage.

Ferrets get such joy out of their banditry, however, that it is almost cruel not to allow them access to safe things they can pilfer and hide. Cat toys or small stuffed animals are good options. Always secure anything dangerous and keep valuables out of sight and out of ferret mind.

Block all possible escape routes. Small holes under sinks and cupboards that could lead to the outside, dryer and air-conditioning vents, and, of course, windows and doors are all potential paths to freedom and disaster. More than one ferret owner has lost a ferret through a small hole around a pipe, through an unsecured screen, or through a dryer vent. Ferrets can easily chew through plastic dryer tubing (often a dryer vent is a desired hiding place for ferreted objects) and in a few short moments escape through the vent and into the outside world. Metal tubing is a ferret-proof fix for this potential problem, as is always having a keen awareness of what a ferret is up to.

It goes without saying that owners need to supervise their ferrets constantly, especially around large appliances like washers and dryers. These common household appliances are dangerous, as are refrigerators, dishwashers, and some household furnishings. Many ferret owners have tragically lost a ferret that hid in a load of laundry or tried to crawl up

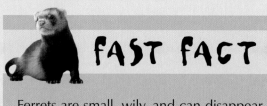

FAST FACT

Ferrets are small, wily, and can disappear in a matter of moments, so it's crucial to keep tabs on your ferret's location. Eventually, a ferret can learn to come when called, but at first try putting a small, breakaway cat collar with a bell on your ferret whenever it is out of its cage.

into the coils of a refrigerator. For that reason, be sure to make large appliances off-limits or to secure the sides, door, and bottom so a curious ferret can't crawl in and into danger.

Furnishings, such as reclining chairs or sofa beds can also be deadly. Ferrets will often easily sneak into or under movable furnishings, only to be crushed when they are sat on or moved. Some ferrets have even been injured by tunneling into the springs of a stationary couch or hiding behind a couch cushion. Be aware of where your pet ferret is at all times, particularly if there are possible danger spots in a home. Many people will actually get rid of these items or move them to parts of the home where the ferret is not allowed access.

Finally, all other possible dangers should be evaluated and moved. Potentially poisonous plants, household chemicals, garbage cans, and medications should always be kept far out of a ferret's reach. It only takes a few moments for curious ferrets to get in trouble, so vigilance is a constant job.

Folding, reclining, or swiveling furniture can pose a safety hazard for your ferret. Make sure you know where he is at all times so that he doesn't get hurt.

A FAMILY CONFERENCE: Once the perimeter has been secured, it is time to sit down with family members and discuss the new ferrets—how they are to be handled, and what will happen when they come home. As much as new ferret owners want to cuddle and play with their new pets, it is important to understand that the first few days are not the time to have the entire neighborhood or extended family in for a visit with the new arrival. Ferrets need time to adjust to their new surroundings and quiet handling by their immediate family, with whom they will bond. Young children, especially, need to be taught to treat their new ferrets with care, gentleness, and respect, to avoid injury on both sides. Parents often have practice sessions with a stuffed animal on how to pick up a ferret, touch it, and talk to it. Rules should be established in the ferrets' best interest. Once your ferrets adjust to their new home, there will be plenty of time to introduce new people and to expand play sessions.

QUARANTINE: If you have other ferrets already, prepare a special area for quarantining the new arrivals. Veterinarians recommend that you quarantine new ferrets from existing ones for at least thirty days to help protect the ferrets you already have from diseases possibly being carried by the newcomer. If a new ferret shows any sign of illness, quarantine is not just recommended—it is mandatory, and the ferret should be taken immediately to a veterinarian for examination. Ferrets are susceptible to a wide variety of illnesses, including human flu and colds. Quarantined ferrets should be kept in a separate cage and room, and good hygiene must be practiced in between handling new ferrets and old. Once quarantine is up, the ferret can be gradually introduced to his new housemates.

CREATING HOME SWEET FERRET HOME

Once all preparations are complete, it's time to bring in all the paraphernalia associated with having a pet ferret. As previously discussed, the setup costs for a pet ferret can be quite high, but ferret-keeping can also be done at a relatively reasonable cost. Think in terms of safety, comfort, and practicality instead of frills and flash, especially if budgetary concerns are important. Huge, multilevel ferret condos are available, complete with ramps, hammocks and all sorts of accessories, but in reality a ferret needs only basic, affordable items to make its home. At least 80 percent of the time a ferret spends in their cage, it will be sleeping. Most play will occur outside the cage, particularly if the ferret is given appropriate exercise periods, so having a supersized cage is not essential.

THE CAGE ITSELF: When choosing a cage for one ferret, it should be a minimum of 24-by-24-by-18 inches (61x61x46 cm) in size. Anything less than this would not give the ferret adequate space. Naturally, a cage housing more than one ferret will need to be larger. Cages come in a variety of materials, but most are made of metal wire with a wire or solid floor. A solid floor is preferable because it keeps your ferrets from injuring their paws. If you buy a cage with a wire floor, the floor should be completely covered with soft bedding.

Make sure to buy a cage specified for ferrets or other small animals of a similar size. Ferrets can often escape from dog crates or other cages used

Your ferret should have a cage that is large enough to accommodate both his water and food dishes, as well as a comfortable place to sleep.

to house them. Some people will simply buy a large dog carrier and use this as a den, which is acceptable, provided that it can hold food, water, a litter pan, and places for the ferret to burrow and sleep.

Multilevel cages or condos of various sizes are highly touted, but, from a medical standpoint, they may actually be dangerous. The wire shelves that make up each level are typically connected by ramps or have hammocks strung between them, and ferrets have fallen and injured themselves while navigating these. If you want a multilevel cage, all ramps and shelves should be well padded with soft material that can be removed and laundered. Sports socks that fit around the ramps or material with Velcro attached are ideal for this purpose, although care should be used with Velcro because many ferrets find it an irresistible treat (and, if ingested, it can cause an intestinal blockage). Still, ferret condos are very popular, and many owners consider them well suited to a ferret's playful nature. The truth is that ferrets are burrowers by nature and are just as happy cuddling in a low-strung hammock or sleep sack on the floor of their cage as they are climbing to the heights. Cages should be considered as your ferrets' den, and not their primary playground.

Elaborate setups are unnecessary, as long as the cage is safe, clean, and comfortable.

All cages should be constructed of safe, nonporous materials that can be easily cleaned and disinfected. Large plastic or glass aquarium-style tanks retain humidity and are not appropriate for ferrets. Metal cages should be coated and not galvanized, because ferrets will often nibble on the bars of their cage, and zinc—used in galvanizing—is toxic if swallowed. Avoid painted metal or at least make certain any paint is lead-free.

FERRET DÉCOR: Bedding must be in the cage at all times and should consist of soft fabric and materials. Shavings, paper bedding, and bedding used for other small animals is unnecessary and potentially dangerous. Shavings may contain cedar and pine oils, which are bad for the ferret's respiratory system, and loose, fluffy bedding can be chewed and swallowed. Ferrets prefer to cuddle in soft, fleecy fabrics, which are also a much safer alternative. Ferret bedding can be something as simple as a T-shirt, a soft towel, a blanket, or a hand-stitched sleep sack or hammock. Specially made ferret sleep sacks and hammocks are also available at most pet supply stores. All bedding items should be washable

A ferret snoozes in his fleecy hammock.

and changed frequently, at least once a week for cleanliness and to minimize ferret odor in the cage. Special care does not need to be taken with the laundry as long as it is washed in hot, soapy water and dried thoroughly before being replaced in the cage.

Sleep sacks are highly recommended, as these small, ferret-sized pouches are a ferret favorite. Ferrets love to burrow and snooze in them—they are soft and dark and simulate a natural burrow. While some owners put their ferret's sacks up on a high shelf in their cage, it is actually best to keep them on the floor of the cage so the ferret won't accidentally fall down while sleeping. This also more closely mimics where a ferret or weasel would sleep in the wild, as the phrase "go to ground," an old term referring to a small animal digging and hiding in a hole, illustrates.

THE LITTER BOX: One essential component of a ferret's cage is a litter box. While litter box training takes time, it is important to have a box in the ferret's cage as well as several in various corners of the

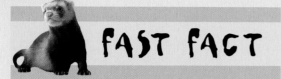

When it comes to sleeping, ferrets are experts. They are such deep sleepers and can be so difficult to awaken that some new ferret owners have been known to panic and think their pet has died, a situation jokingly referred to as "Dead Ferret Syndrome."

house from the very beginning. Ferrets love to perform their toilet duties in corners and are not particular if there is a litter box there or not. When playing, they will simply scoot off to the nearest corner and do their business. To help things along, make sure to provide ample opportunities for them to do the right thing.

Plastic litter boxes shaped especially for corners are available for small animals. These boxes have high sides to accommodate a ferret's tendency to "aim high" and a low front for easy access. It is always a wise idea to line corners and areas under litter boxes with plastic sheeting or towels, as some ferrets prefer to go under, behind, or around the litter box, especially at first. All litter boxes should be scooped and cleaned daily, and litter should consist of hard pellets, such as recycled

newspaper litter or plain unscented kitty litter, as opposed to the more modern clumping varieties.

FOOD AND WATER: Food and water are obviously essential and must be available at all times. Water can be provided in either a hanging bottle or in a bowl on the floor. Many ferrets adapt quickly and easily to a water bottle or may have been used to it in their previous cage. If you're using a bowl, choose one that is heavy and difficult to tip or one with clips that attach to the side of the cage. Ceramic bowls work best for ferrets. An unsecured lightweight bowl will quickly become a splash toy for a ferret. Avoid metal bowls with rubber bottoms, as ferrets will often overturn the bowl anyway and then feast on the rubber for good measure, with

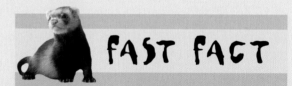

When choosing litter, safety and cleanliness are paramount. Regular gravel litter and pellet litters, such as heat-treated feline pine litters, corncob litters, and recycled newspaper litters, are best. Clumping litters and certain untreated pine and cedar litters are dangerous to ferrets. If your ferret seems inclined to eat a certain type of litter, try a different kind.

THE OUTDOOR FERRET

Not all ferrets live indoors. While typical ferret owners house their pets inside, some, especially in warmer climates, do not. In some parts of the world, especially the British Isles, ferrets still live in cozy setups in backyard gardens, especially those that are used for hunting and breeding.

In general, the best place to keep an outside ferret's cage is on a porch, in an enclosed lanai, or in another protected area. It is essential to shelter the ferret from the elements and to avoid exposing this creature to temperatures below 20° Fahrenheit (-6° Celsius) or above 90°F (32°C). Ferrets do not do well in extreme heat, and can easily become overheated.

Owners also need to secure the cage against predators and possible escape. In many parts of the United States, coyotes are becoming a huge problem, causing the death of many outdoor pets, even those in cages.

Remember that ferrets kept outdoors need the same socialization opportunities and time outside their cage as indoor ferrets do, and they also need extra attention when it comes to parasite control. In warm climates, outdoor ferrets should be kept on both heartworm and flea prevention protocols year round.

---

potentially deadly consequences. Avoid unsecured plastic bowls for both food and water. They are too lightweight, and can become fun and messy ferret toys.

WHERE TO PLACE YOUR FERRET'S HOME: Ferrets like their dark quiet holes, but they are social animals at heart. So when it comes time to choose a spot for the ferret's cage, place it near where the family spends a lot of time and where there is normal household activity. While a back bedroom isn't ideal, neither is right next to the television or stereo.

Try to find an out-of-the-way corner of a central room or a place adjacent to a central room, where the ferret can interact with the household as it eats, grooms itself, and engages in any waking activity that doesn't take place outside its cage.

A NEW BEGINNING

The day your new ferret comes home is a day of firsts. It is the first day the ferret is coming into contact with its new owner. Sometimes it is the first time the ferret has been riding in a car or away from its littermates or companions. For many ferret owners, it's the first time they've ever been around a ferret for any length of time or, in some cases, the first pet they've ever had. So both owners and ferret will go through an adjustment period. This time can either be a fun, learning experience or set the stage for future problems. Getting things right from the beginning is the key to a happy, healthy ferret and ensures that a new home becomes a forever home.

For the first hours and days, the new ferret should be handled gently, patiently, and quietly. Even a calm, well-ordered home can be scary under certain circumstances. A new ferret may be overwhelmed by its surroundings, so you need to take some appropriate precautions. Keep in mind that this first day is only the beginning of a long and hopefully happy relationship between ferret and owner. There is plenty of time for wild play and excitement later on. The first day is not the time for show and tell with the entire neighborhood or a

rousing game of chase-the-weasel with the family dog.

A new ferret should be treated with patience and given space and time to explore its new environment. As soon as your ferret arrives at home, place it securely in its cage. This gives it time to rest and regroup. In no time at all, you'll see your ferret's head poking out inquisitively to check out all the exciting things in its new home—a sure sign of settling in. Once the ferret is relaxed, it is all right to start bringing it out, perhaps restricting its

Before you know it, your ferret will be anxious to explore his new home!

explorations to just one completely ferret-proofed room, with a few family members in attendance instead of the entire clan.

A PERIOD OF ADJUSTMENT

As the first few days turn into weeks and then months, a ferret will adjust and gradually become a regular member of the family. Often, a new ferret will fit fairly seamlessly into a home, especially if it is an adult.

Kits, however, like puppies or kittens, will go through a period of adjustment, testing the rules and exhibiting over-the-top rambunctious behavior. All ferrets are playful and inquisitive, but kits have often not been socialized enough to know the difference between good and bad ferret behavior. Kits are more likely to nip during rough play—not out of meanness, but because they don't know any better.

Biting is a common way two kits play together and this behavior is normal for them. Most kits haven't learned that human skin is made of thinner, weaker stuff than that of their ferret playmates. Frequent handling, gentle correction, and patience are crucial at this point.

Ferrets should never be disciplined roughly or put back in their cage as punishment. The best response to misbehavior is to cor-rect your ferret with a gentle "No," and then step away from the situation. Put the ferret on the floor and move away, an effective time-out that will soon give it the message that biting equals an abrupt halt to playtime.

PLAYTIME

As part of playtime, kits and adults alike will explore and investigate their home environment. This is the time when pens, credit cards, watches, and all manner of exciting things will begin to disappear as a ferret spirits them away to its favorite hiding place. You need to take extra care and not let your guard down once the first few days are past.

Ferrets can get in just as much trouble (and perhaps even more) in an environment they are familiar with, because their self-confidence has blossomed. Keep in mind that no

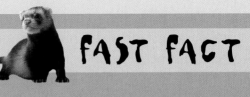

FAST FACT

Ferrets love holidays (all those gifts!), and special care needs to be taken with ferret-proofing during this time. Keep holiday plants away from ferrets, make sure to leave the bottom portion of a tree free of lights and decorations, and avoid using icicles and small ornaments that could be easily swallowed.

When you allow your curious acrobatic friend to explore his new home, keep an eye on him to make sure he doesn't get into too much trouble!

matter how long ferrets have been present in a home, it is never safe to leave them out of their cage unattended.

LITTER BOX TRAINING

Litter box training becomes either a triumph or a struggle at this point. Most ferrets adjust over time to using a box regularly, but almost all ferrets have an occasional accident. Kits, especially, need lots of practice using a box and lots of opportunity to do so. Be sure to put several boxes in the play area, so it is easier for your ferret to handle his sanitary needs properly.

THE FIRST VET VISIT

Make sure your new ferret has a thorough medical checkup and any necessary vaccines. This is also the time to build a relationship with a veterinarian. Not only is this important from the standpoint of your ferret's health, but it is an opportunity

for your ferret to become used to certain routines, to develop its socialization skills, and to become used to being handled outside the comfort and safety of its home.

GROWING AND CHANGING

Changes don't stop once a ferret has successfully completed the first few weeks or months of adjustment to its new home. Kits grow up into adults, older ferrets continue to become more social, and both develop their own unique personalities. Some ferrets are more playful, some prefer a cuddle to a romp, and each ferret will find a special way to engage the hearts of its owners.

As kits grow, they lose a small—very small—amount of their initial energy. They are still playful and fun, but they become a bit less wild as they mature. Most kits also undergo changes in their appearance. The mask of a ferret develops with age, and often, the ferret's coat color deepens or lightens. Color changes are actually common throughout life. A ferret's coat will often change from dark to light, based on the season, and all ferrets typically shed twice a year.

Most ferrets mature into adults at around eight months of age, although, of course, with ferrets, age is only a number. Ferrets go through life with the exuberance of the average human two-year-old, and this sense of fun and mischief is part of what makes them such delightful companions.

SOCIALIZING AND SOCIALIZATION

Throughout life, ferrets exhibit their natural curiosity and joie de vivre. Ferrets need daily interaction with their people, so you have to find new ways to challenge them and keep them occupied. New toys, fun games, and all sorts of other activities can bring owners and ferrets closer together, and the bond between pet and owner should only grow stronger over time.

Socializing ferrets from day one is the key to a healthy, lifelong attachment. At first, just one or maybe two people should handle and acquaint themselves with the ferret. Children, particularly small children, will want to handle the pet immediately, but this kind of interaction should wait. First, teach children how to properly handle the ferret, as well as how to protect the ferret from their well-meaning, but

DECLAWING: NOT AN OPTION FOR FERRETS

Ferrets are natural diggers and scratchers. They love to dig into carpet, furnishings, and wood objects like doorframes, and their sharp nails can sometimes scratch sensitive human skin. To human families, this behavior can be very destructive, but ferrets are just following their natural instincts.

Cats that exhibit these behaviors are often declawed. Declawing of cats is a surgical procedure that is becoming increasingly controversial in many areas. Ferrets, however, should never, ever be declawed.

Ferret nails do not retract, and removing the nail actually removes a large part of the ferret's toe. Declawing is considered inhumane by both animal lovers and veterinarians, and leaves the ferret crippled and in pain.

The best way to prevent accidental scratching of people by ferrets is to trim a ferret's nails frequently. Keep destruction within limits by restricting a ferret's access to certain rooms and by protecting furniture and carpeting with thick plastic.

When choosing a ferret as a pet, you need to recognize that they are never going to be as well behaved as the average dog. Ferrets do not mean any harm by their actions, but, sadly, many ferrets are surrendered to shelters every year by owners who had unrealistic expectations.

inadvertently dangerous, exuberance. Once a ferret is comfortable with being handled, it is time to introduce the ferret to other family members and for children to become familiar with handling it.

This process may take some time, but very soon the ferret will be snuggling up with family members and bonding, a reward of its own for your initial patience. At first, let the ferret take the lead when it comes to snuggling, remembering that your ferret also wants to explore its new environment, something it can do best by play. Have toys and hiding holes available from the beginning, and, of course, make sure several litter boxes are accessible and that the ferret is shown their location. Don't wait until the ferret is worn out to put it back in its cage. Try a half hour to an hour of socialization at a time at the outset, then take a break. If the ferret seems ready for more, bring it out again.

GETTING TO KNOW OTHER PETS

Wait until later to introduce Fido or the family cat to the ferret. Once the ferret is familiar with the people in their new home, it is all right to move on to other pets. This should be done with caution and always under direct supervision.

Ferrets are typically responsive to new ferrets coming into the household and after a short introductory period will often snuggle down for a cuddle or begin to play. There can be rough play or struggles for dominance at first, particularly with males, but usually they adapt fairly easily.

Cats are often completely oblivious to ferrets, but should still be closely watched. Dogs may do best on a leash so owners can rein them in if they become overexcited. Allow time for nonconfrontational observation and for the animals to become acquainted with new smells before bringing dog and ferret together. Then, slowly introduce them, standing ready to intervene, if needed. If there seems to be any indication that a dog will attack a ferret, don't risk it.

With time, most family pets adjust to their ferret brother or sister. Nonetheless, ferrets should never be left unattended with any other animal, for safety's sake. Small pocket pets, such as hamsters, mice, birds, and even lizards and snakes, should never be introduced to ferrets or trusted alone with them, even if the animals are in a tank or a cage. Ferrets are smart, wily, and agile and can easily dislodge the top of a tank or open a cage door. More than one ferret owner has lost another family pet due to the ferret's keen hunting instinct,

Your ferret and cat could become good friends—but until they are used to each other, don't let them be alone together.

including good-sized birds, rabbits, and snakes. Remember, ferrets were bred to hunt small rodents, and weasels are renowned for their ability to capture and dispatch snakes, birds, and other prey. As previously discussed, anyone with small pets might think twice about bringing a ferret into his home. At the very least, keep small pets well-secured and far out of a curious ferret's reach.

CHAPTER FIVE

Caring For Your Ferret

Pet ferrets need a proper place to live, but they also need proper care. A ferret's needs are relatively simple, but fulfilling them can be difficult, especially at first. Love, shelter, food, and water are easily provided, but ferrets also need to be groomed, exercised, and trained to be good citizens.

Ferrets are sometimes difficult to train. They are also wiggly creatures that often resent brushing or bathing when they would rather be playing. Taking care of a ferret is an exercise in patience and living with a ferret is an exercise in hard work and commitment, rewarding though it may be.

Feeding your ferret a balanced, protein-rich diet will help to keep him healthy.

NUTRITION

Whether adults or kits, when ferrets first come to a home, they will likely already be accustomed to eating commercially prepared ferret food. Kits are typically weaned by the age of six weeks and are not sold until they are on solid food. Kits also eat the same food as adult ferrets, and special care need not be taken when feeding them, unless they refuse their food. Lack of appetite is sometimes an early a sign of disease, and any ferret that stops eating should immediately be taken to a veterinarian for examination to make sure that the ferret's refusal to eat doesn't indicate a bigger problem. For new ferrets, sometimes the cause is simply stress, and a little supplement added to

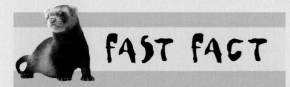

FAST FACT

When your new ferrets come home, keep them on the diet they have been eating. Dietary changes, if needed, can come later. Any time ferrets have their food switched, it should be done over several weeks, gradually increasing the amount of new food mixed with old until they are completely on the new food. Switching a food quickly can lead to hunger strikes or diarrhea.

the daily ration will improve their appetite immediately.

Ferrets are carnivores and require a meat-based diet. They cannot digest vegetable or plant matter well, and it should very rarely be fed to them, even if they appear to enjoy it. Vegetable consumption may lead to nutritional problems as well as health concerns, including bladder stones. Either commercial ferret food or high-quality kitten food provides the nutritional balance that a ferret needs. Dog food and adult cat food should not be used. While some advocate home cooking for ferrets, this is not recommended. It is too difficult to strike the proper balance of nutrients, not to mention time-consuming, messy, and expensive.

Commercial ferret diets are high in fat and protein and low in carbohydrates. Excessive carbohydrate intake by ferrets has been linked to health problems and obesity and is not nutritionally necessary. At the minimum, a ferret's diet should contain between 18 and 30 percent fat and 30–40 percent protein. Most commercial ferret diets meet these standards. Ferret food usually comes in the form of dry pellets or kibble. Canned or wet food is available, but is messy, causes smellier stools, and is bad for a ferret's teeth. In the wild, weasels eat insects, small animals, and birds, and the natural cartilage and bones help keep their teeth sharp and clean. By contrast, wet food clings to the teeth and lacks the benefits of hard, crunchy kibble.

When measuring out food, follow the recommendations on the side of the bag. Bored ferrets may overeat, and, if not exercised properly, can become overweight, a risk factor for insulinoma (see Chapter 6). Treats should be limited, though ferrets love them, and it can be hard to say no. Many treats are available in pet stores, and some are better than others. Look for treats with meat as the primary ingredient. Chicken baby food, toddler meat sticks, and unprocessed lunch meat are great treats as well.

Not all treats are good treats. While ferrets love apples, raisins, and the like, give these to them in very small quantities, if at all. Raisins should be limited as they are high in sugar and can lead to dental decay. They have also been found to be toxic to dogs and cats, and it is unknown if ferrets have a similar reaction to them. Apples and other hard fruits can cause an intestinal blockage if too large a piece is swallowed and should be given only in tiny pieces or mashed. Small servings

"RAW" DIET PROS AND CONS

Weasels and other wild relatives of ferrets are carnivores and survive on a diet made up of insects, birds, rodents, and other small prey. In the United States and other countries, especially in Europe, a "raw" diet consisting of whole small animals, as well as raw meat, is becoming much more common for domesticated ferrets. High in protein and fat, low in carbohydrates, raw diets are thought to be healthier than processed foods.

But there are public health concerns involved in feeding your ferret a raw diet, including the risk of parasites and bacterial infections. Ferrets are not like their wild cousins, in that they lack some of the immunity that wild animals develop as a result of constant exposure to pathogens.

It is also important to remember that humans do not normally handle the feces of wild animals, but they do clean ferrets' litter boxes on a daily basis. Any bacteria or parasites a ferret encounters can be directly passed to its human family and possibly be a cause of disease. This is a concern for people with a compromised immune system, the elderly, and children. As a result, most veterinarians don't recommend feeding a ferret or any domestic pet a raw diet for these reasons.

of soft fruits, such as mashed bananas, are probably a safer bet. Avoid treats such as cereal or crackers that are high in carbohydrates or feed them in strict moderation. Make sure to keep unintentional treats, such as dairy, chocolate, candy, or medications, far from a ferret's reach. Treats should represent only a small portion of a ferret's diet. They are best kept for rewards, training, or unpleasant tasks like nail clipping. Instead of letting ferrets gorge on treats, give them plenty of dry kibble.

Vitamin supplements are optional, especially if a ferret is eating good-quality food. Most ferrets, however, will benefit from a coat supplement that is high in essential fatty acids. These supplements are typically quite tasty and can be obtained at pet stores or from veterinarians. Most ferrets think of them as a treat, and they help your ferret stay sleek and shiny.

Ferrets snack throughout the day. They have a fast metabolism and will eat small amounts every few hours. Make sure food is fresh and left out so your ferrets can eat whenever they want. When it comes time to put new food in the bowl, throw out whatever is left over. Leftover ferret

food will quickly go bad, due to its high fat content.

Also make certain that the ferret has a constant source of fresh water. It is wise to provide both a water bottle and a heavy bowl of water in case one source spills or gets plugged up. Keep food and water close together; ferrets like to eat and drink in tandem. Also keep dishes at the opposite end of the cage from the litter box. Ferrets don't like to eat or sleep close to where they eliminate, and this arrangement also makes sense for sanitary reasons.

EXERCISE

Exercise for ferrets is better known as play, play, play. Activity comes easily

Ferret exercise comes in the form of play, and your guy will be ready to play at a moment's notice.

to the ferret (when they aren't sleeping, of course), and all ferrets need daily exercise for their physical and mental well-being. This can take the form of play, socialization, games, or even excursions to the outside world.

The watchword for any ferrets that are out of their cage is safety. Before taking ferrets out for playtime, do a quick sweep of their play area for potential dangers. Most homes with ferrets as pets are already ferret-proofed, but it only takes one forgotten pencil eraser to turn a leisurely weekend into a protracted visit at the emergency vet. If you plan to take your ferrets outside your home, make sure that harnesses and collars are escape-proof.

At least several hours out of each day should be designated as ferret playtime. Ferrets need between two and four hours to run around, socialize, and get into as much trouble (or try to) as their little hearts desire. This should be a special time for both owner and ferret.

Try to time play sessions for when a ferret is naturally most active. Ferrets like to be up and about at dawn and dusk. While the early morning hours might not fit most people's schedules, the majority of owners find late afternoon or early evening a good time to take their fuzzy out of its cage.

The only limits to play are an owner's imagination, and often the ferret will be the one to come up with new and innovative activities. Chase, tug-of-war, crawling through tunnels, digging in specially designed ferret dig boxes, hiding games, and playing with toys are all tried-and-true ferret favorites. Some ferrets enjoy swimming for fun, in a little pool or tub (under supervision, of course) and others like hunting for treats in a maze. Almost any activity is a joy when a ferret is involved.

If it's a nice day—not too hot and not too cold—consider going for a walk. Many ferrets enjoy investigating the outside world while on a harness and leash. First make sure that ferrets are not prohibited outside by local ordinance, and once outside, keep a close eye and hand on the ferret at all times. Walking ferrets isn't exactly vigorous exercise. It's more of an occasion for them to romp, sniff, and explore. Still, this can be invigorating for both owner and ferret and is bound to be a conversation starter with the neighbors. Don't expect to go far—a few houses down the block or the boundaries of their own yard are usually far enough—but the opportunity to romp in fall leaves, dig in a flower bed, or just have the breeze blowing in their fur is as good as a trip to the park for most ferrets.

Ferrets love to explore new places. While a ferret will not walk around the block on a leash like a dog, a leash will help keep your ferret pal under control while he explores.

Inside, toys take a prominent role in ferret playtime. Almost anything can be a toy, as long as it is safe, ferret-proof, and fun. Toys can be either bought or homemade. Even a paper bag can be a source of endless amusement for a ferret. Try to have lots of different toys on hand, as ferrets love to mix things up and are stimulated by variety.

GROOMING

Unlike a dog of similar size, ferrets don't need much primping or pampering. While saving on grooming bills is a plus, don't think that grooming and coat care aren't neces-sary. All ferrets need grooming in some form, including regular brushing, nail trims, ear cleaning, and the occasional bath. Grooming is not intensive or time-consuming, but it is often made difficult by the ferret's inherent wiggly nature. The best grooming tools are a patient nature and the occasional well-timed bribe. Treats or supplements like Ferretone or hairball paste can distract a ferret just when things are looking dicey.

COAT CARE: The most basic form of ferret grooming is proper brushing. Ferrets have thick, heavy, greasy coats and will self-groom several times a day. This self-grooming distributes the oil throughout their coats, but it also can lead to ingestion of large amounts of hair. Each time a ferret licks its fur, it swallows a little hair. Hair that accumulates in the stomach can lead to intestinal blockage. Frequent brushing will decrease this risk.

Ferrets need brushing at least several times a week with a soft-bristled brush, a special ferret brush, or a flea comb. Brushing is best done when a ferret is tired from play. Brushing before playtime is generally an exercise in futility, as your fuzzy displays a restless, hard-to-hold streak. The strokes should go in the direction of hair growth, from head to tail. Don't forget to brush the tail, as well as gently stroking the chest and tummy.

Extra brushing is necessary during spring and fall when ferrets are shedding their coats. In spring, ferrets have

an exceptionally heavy shed as they are getting rid of their thick winter coat. At that time of year, ferrets will lose huge chunks of undercoat at a time or "blow" their undercoat. This is a prime time for hairballs, so brush daily or strip away clumps of blown coat. They should pull out easily in soft, fuzzy chunks. If they don't, don't force them; gently work them out with a comb or brush.

Another aspect of coat care is supplements. Several products are available on the market, including fatty acid supplements, such as Ferretone and Linatone. Ferretone is available at most pet stores and comes in liquid or specially formulated treats. It is designed for ferrets, as opposed to Linatone, which is designed for dogs. Either one can be given to make the coat thicker and shinier. Advocates recommend giving it daily, but every other day administration will likely have the same effect. Ferrets find the supplements very tasty and they can be given as a treat to assist in bonding. Contrary to label directions, it is recommended to administer the liquid on a spoon and have the ferret lick it, rather than pouring it directly on the food.

Use a soft brush on your ferret's coat regularly. This will help remove excess fur and prevent hairballs.

Soaking dry food in oil tends to make it mushy and increases spoilage.

Supplements for hairball prevention, such as Ferret-lax or Laxatone, are also available. These pastes are thick and sticky and have a petroleum base. They ease the passage of hair through the intestinal tract and should be administered a few times a week or every other day during shedding season.

DENTAL CARE: The first step in good dental care is feeding ferrets a nutritionally balanced, dry ferret food. Crunchy kibble helps prevent plaque buildup and sound nutrition keeps teeth strong. Ferrets are very prone to dental disease, including dental plaque, tartar, and loose or infected teeth. Sugary treats and wet food will only compound this problem. Beyond diet, proper dental care involves tooth brushing at home and professional veterinary cleaning.

Tooth brushing needn't be an everyday event to be effective. Most ferrets will benefit from tooth brushing two to three times weekly, although daily is ideal. The only tools needed are a small, child-sized or pet toothbrush and a strong will. Pet toothpaste is helpful but optional.

TOOTH CLEANING: CALL THE PROFESSIONAL

Ferrets are prone to dental problems. Loose or infected teeth can cause pain, weight loss from not eating, systemic infections, and disease in other parts of the body as the infection spreads. Keeping the teeth and gums healthy is now recognized as an important part of preventing heart, kidney, and liver disease in both people and animals. A professional tooth cleaning becomes necessary when tartar accumulates, when dental and gum disease is present, or when brushing is not an option. Teeth cleaning should only be done at the office of a licensed veterinarian. Some laypeople and pet groomers attempt dental cleanings, but this is dangerous and often against the law.

Only veterinarians can administer the anesthetic necessary to make cleaning painless and safe, and only they have the knowledge to examine the teeth and gums to assess their overall health. Veterinarians will often do blood work before the procedure to make sure the ferret is healthy. Anesthetic is then administered, and the ferret will sleep through the procedure, which includes ultrasonic cleaning, polishing, and any necessary extractions.

The main goal of brushing a ferret's teeth is to loosen the soft plaque that accumulates, particularly on the back teeth and canines. This plaque will eventually harden into tartar, which leads to gum disease.

Use a wet toothbrush and a small amount of pet toothpaste, if desired. Pet toothpaste is usually meat-flavored, tasty, and can make the brushing experience more enjoyable for the ferret. Most pastes available from veterinarians also contain enzymes to break down plaque. Never use human toothpaste or anything with fluoride, as even small amounts of these products are toxic to ferrets. Brush in a gentle up-and-down or circular motion. A few repetitions are sufficient. Try to clean the back teeth especially, even though this can be difficult. Rinsing is not necessary.

Most ferrets won't sit still for tooth brushing. There are several positions or tricks that make this procedure go more easily. Try flipping the ferret on its back and holding it gently in between your knees while using your hands to open the mouth and brush. If an assistant is available, have one person gently scruff the ferret and hold it up so its body hangs down.

To scruff a ferret, gather the loose skin at the back of the neck and shoulders between the fingers and thumb and pull up, avoiding pulling too tightly or digging in with your fingernails. This skin is thick and greatly desensitized at this point, like a cat's, and most ferrets do not mind this at all. Mother ferrets carry their young around by the scruff. Scruffing gives you excellent control of the head and neck and almost always makes the ferret compliant. It does not hurt. The position is relaxing, and most ferrets will yawn almost immediately, giving great access to the back teeth.

Make sure to brush confidently and quickly, as most ferrets won't stick around too long. Try to make brushing a relaxing time and always wait to do it until after your ferret is tired from play. If tooth brushing turns into a battle, it will become an

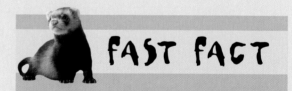

FAST FACT

Like other mammals, ferrets are born with baby teeth that fall out as their permanent teeth begin to come in. Permanent teeth come at around two months, starting in the front and working around the back. Adult ferrets typically have about thirty-four permanent teeth, most of which are adapted for tearing and crushing food as opposed to chewing.

odious chore and one that is likely to be neglected.

BATHING: Frequent bathing of a ferret is unnecessary. At the most, ferrets should be bathed perhaps once or twice a month. Excessive bathing makes a ferret's skin and coat become dry and itchy. Ferrets that are bathed too frequently may actually have an increased odor, as their skin responds to dryness by producing more oil. Most ferrets need only an occasional bath every few months unless they get into something messy or sticky, but many people find that once-a-month bathing decreases a ferret's musky smell and helps make it a more pleasant companion.

Many ferrets enjoy a bath. Where to bathe a ferret is completely up to the ferret and the owner. Some ferrets will happily swim in a tub, whereas others will find a quick dip in the sink or a plastic dishpan all they can tolerate. No matter where they are bathed, never leave a ferret unattended in water for any period of time.

Fill the sink or tub with a small amount of water, then gently submerge the ferret, being careful not to dunk it completely. Once it is wet, apply a small amount of shampoo

Some ferrets enjoy an occasional bath. Mild shampoo that can be used to clean a ferret's coat properly can be purchased at a pet supply store.

and lather, especially around the tail and head where the oil glands are most prominent. Take great care to avoid getting shampoo in the ferret's eyes, which can cause discomfort or even ulceration. A small amount of artificial tear ointment can help protect the eyes and reduce discomfort.

Choose a soap-free shampoo made for ferrets or kittens. Human baby shampoo, while safe, isn't the appropriate pH for ferret skin. Never use shampoos with flea products in them. Flea shampoos that are safe for kittens are usually safe for ferrets, but bathing a ferret with flea shampoo isn't necessary with all the flea preventatives available today. Ferrets may have a serious reaction to the chemicals in flea shampoo, and it is better to be safe than sorry. For that same reason, never use dog flea collars, drops, shampoos, or sprays on a ferret. They are toxic and lethal.

Once the ferret is clean, rinse it thoroughly. Leftover shampoo that isn't rinsed off can make the skin dry and itchy. At this point, a conditioner can be applied and rinsed off, if desired. Some ferrets might enjoy splashing around in the water for a bit after they are clean. After the bath, get them out and dry them thoroughly in a towel. Be sure to hang on; most ferrets will try to get away immediately. Once they're

toweled off, let them loose and prepare for a monster truck rally of ferret proportions as they run around, go crazy, and try to rub off the scent of the bath on any available piece of rug or furniture. It is a good idea to make sure to switch bedding at the same time a ferret is bathed so a clean ferret doesn't go right back into a dirty, smelly cage.

NAIL CARE: Clipping a ferret's nails is right up there next to washing windows on most people's unpleasant chores list. This task is important, however, as ferret nails will grow long and sharp if not trimmed. In the wild, weasels dig constantly, wearing down their nails. In a home, nails will grow and grow and scratch and scratch—owners, furniture, doors, and everything else. A ferret's nails can get caught in furniture and be torn off, causing injury and pain to the ferret. How often a ferret needs

FAST FACT

The earlier a ferret starts having its nails clipped the better. A kit will quickly become used to regular nail trims and will grow up into an adult that cooperates with nail trimming instead of hiding when the trimmers come out.

its nails trimmed depends on how fast they grow. Some ferrets need weekly trims; others only need them every few months.

To clip a ferret's nails, use a sharp nail trimmer. A small human nail clipper or a cat nail trimmer is ideal. First try trimming your ferret's nails while it is sleeping. Ferrets are surprisingly deep sleepers and the task can often be accomplished quickly and with little fuss. If a ferret is awake, it's best to have an assistant hold it. Here's the best way: Have your assistant put one hand under the ferret's chest and hold the ferret close to her body with the inside curve of her elbow. She should use her other hand to keep the ferret's head and neck still. Difficult ferrets can be scruffed.

The nail has two parts—the hard outer claw and the pulpy inner layer or "quick." The claw is made up of keratin. Keratin is dead tissue with no nerve endings and is painless to clip. The quick is living tissue: It is blood-rich, has a nerve supply, and is very painful if cut. The quick appears on most ferret nails as a pink line within the white claw, just above the tapered portion of the nail. If the ferret has dark nails, the quick cannot be seen.

When cutting your ferret's nails, only cut the white portion of the nail. Do not cut the quick. It is usually safe to cut dark nails just at the very tip, but not always. If a ferret has dark nails, ask a veterinarian or another professional to demonstrate nail trims and how to avoid the quick.

Holding the nail clipper in one hand, immobilize the ferret's foot with the other. Ferret claws don't retract like a cat's and are easy to clip. Trim the nail only and continue on through the rest of the toes.

Accidents can happen. Even with caution a ferret can jerk back or the nail clipper can slip. If the quick is nicked, the nail will bleed, and the ferret may panic. Stay calm and

Nail clipping can be a challenge at first, but remain patient. Your ferret just needs to get used to the process.

immediately put pressure on the nail, then apply a styptic pencil, flour, cornstarch, or a bar of soap to the cut end until the bleeding stops. Most ferrets and owners will be anxious about nail trims after this happens. If nail trimming is too stressful, most veterinary offices will do it for a nominal fee.

EAR CARE: One final grooming task ferrets need is regular ear cleaning. Ferrets regularly accumulate a reddish-brown wax in their ears that can be itchy. The best way to clean a ferret's ears is to hold the ferret the same way you do for nail trims. Take a small amount of ear wash (available at veterinary clinics or pet stores) that is safe for ferrets and squeeze it directly into the ears. Gently rub the ears and let the ferret shake its head. Once this is done, use a cotton swab to gently remove excess wax from the visible portion of the ear. To prevent serious injury, never put a swab inside a ferret's ear. Ear cleaning should be done a few times a month, less frequently if a ferret does not produce a large amount of wax.

TRAINING

Training ferrets is a bit like training overactive toddlers. Sometimes they'll listen, sometimes they won't.

Ferrets won't win any obedience challenges, but they can be taught the basics, as well as household rules and how to use a litter box. While a cat will use a litter box from a very young age, ferrets are more difficult to persuade, and training requires patience. Ferrets can also learn to respond to their name and will sometimes perform tricks for treats. Treats are an important part of any ferret training regimen. When it comes to the average ferret, never underestimate the power of bribery.

LITTER BOX TRAINING: In an ideal world, ferrets would sashay up to their litter box, use it, and be on their way. Unfortunately, ferrets tend to aim a little to the left of ideal, particularly in the bathroom arena. Ferrets may use the box, or they may hit the floor just next to it. They'll also scatter litter around and wipe their rears on the floor for good measure, just to keep things clean, of course.

Start litter box training from day one. The first step is to provide a litter box in the ferret's cage. A corner-shaped box works best. Place your ferret in the box and let him sniff around. Some ferrets will immediately squat; most won't. If a ferret uses a spot next to the box instead, clean up the mess with a paper towel and put it in the box. Sometimes all it

With work, you can train a ferret to do his business in the litter box. You may need to place several litterboxes throughout your home to make going to the bathroom convenient.

takes is a little reminder of what, exactly, the box is for.

If this doesn't work, the next step is to give the ferret as many opportunities to use the box as possible. For example, ferrets like to use the toilet right after they wake up. Keep an eye on a sleeping ferret and, as soon as it's awake, plop it in the box. Repeat this process as many times as necessary. Sooner or later—success! This is where a well-timed bribe comes in. As soon as the ferret uses the box, give it a tasty treat. A reward for a job well done speeds the training process along.

It is relatively easy to train ferrets to use the litter box in their cage. Ferrets don't like to soil their food or bedding, so the box is the obvious place to go. The great wide world is another matter. While outside their cage, ferrets will have to learn to use a box somewhere else. This can be difficult. During playtime, busy ferrets won't run back to their cage to use the proper facility. In fact, they often won't run across a room. To a ferret, any convenient corner is a great place to back up, give a bit of a wiggle, and go. Anticipating nature's call is difficult, but one way to encourage good behavior is by making sure your ferret doesn't leave its cage until it's used the box, especially at first. Once this is done, be alert for future signs that a ferret needs to go.

As soon as a ferret starts to sidle over to a corner with a bit of a wiggle and a tail lift, scoop it up and plop it in the nearest box. Repeat. Bribe your ferret if necessary. Priming the box with feces or urine is also a brilliant idea. Frequent scooping of dirty litter boxes gives them your ferret's seal of approval.

Keep in mind that a single litter box in a playroom is woefully inadequate, particularly if it is a large room. The ferret should have at least one box in each room it plays in, with two for larger rooms. If the ferret seems to prefer a bare corner as opposed to the one the box is in, move the box. It is also wise to protect any carpeting around the box with towels or pieces of plastic. Spare corners that receive the occasional ferret dousing are also good candidates for a bit of protective lining.

With time, patience, and repetition, most ferrets will learn to use a litter box. Of course, the occasional accident will still happen. It is unrealistic to expect perfection, but ferrets will usually behave properly if they are consistently given the opportunity. Of course, a yummy treat for good behavior never hurts.

OTHER KINDS OF TRAINING: For the average ferret owner, the most important aspects of training revolve around the litter box. After that, training is mostly a matter of convenience, tricks, and responsible behavior. Most ferrets can learn to respond to either the sound of their name or some other noise, such as a squeaking toy. Consistent use of treats and constant repetition are necessary to train a ferret to come when called. Having ferrets that will come on command can be a lifesaver if they are lost or if they need to be found in a hurry. Don't ever use a signal to summon ferrets for something unpleasant, such as medicating or putting them away in their cage, though. Keep it fun and rewarding; otherwise, they'll soon stop coming when called.

The same technique of teach and reward can be used for any number of ferret tricks. Sitting up, rolling over, and other antics can be taught with infinite patience and a good amount of Ferretone.

Ferrets shouldn't be punished for misbehavior beyond a stern "No" and the occasional time-out. Any physical punishment will make your ferret fearful and withdrawn. The best way to prevent damage to carpets, upholstery, and other items is to set limits on where a ferret can and can't go in a house. Keep dangerous rooms off-limits. Next, protect doors, carpets, and sofas with the judicious use of plastic covers or gates. Ferrets are determined and, often, once they've found a place where they like to dig, they'll continue doing so. A plastic runner or chair mat can protect floors, or carpet remnants can be laid over problem spots. Protect doors with Plexiglas insets or ferret gates. If all else fails, keep valuable furnishings out of a ferret's reach. Remember, ferrets are animals. Digging, stealing, burrowing, and hiding are natural instincts for them, not deliberate attempts to be bad.

Another problem behavior is nipping. Young ferrets are natural nippers, a behavior made worse by

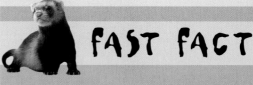

FAST FACT

One of the most common ferret behavior problems is biting. Some ferrets simply nip in play, but others—particularly those that are improperly socialized or who were mistreated in the past—may be more aggressive biters. You can generally alleviate biting by gentle, frequent handling, but if biting is unmanageable, ask the ferret's veterinarian for some other behavior modification technique.

rough handling or play. If a ferret nips, it should be told "No" in as stern a voice as possible and immediately put in a time-out on the floor and away from the owner. Most ferrets quickly learn that biting equals a suspension of play. And what fun, after all, is that?

The key things to remember when training a ferret are patience and consistency. All ferrets can be trained to be better companions. It's up to the individual owner to make this training a success.

CHAPTER SIX

Your Ferret's Health

Few things have as profound an impact on a ferret's well-being as good-quality health care. Vaccinations, preventatives, and timely checkups are all essential to lengthening a ferret's lifespan. The first step is to find a skilled, compassionate veterinarian.

CHOOSING A VETERINARIAN

When looking for a veterinarian, be particular. Not all veterinarians treat

When you are searching for a veterinarian, don't be afraid to call the office and ask questions. Ideally, you want to find a veterinarian with experience treating exotic pets like ferrets.

ferrets or have experience with them, and ferrets are not like smaller versions of cats or dogs. They are a distinct species with special health care requirements and concerns. Ask other ferret owners, neighbors, or friends which veterinarian cares for their pets and why they like this particular vet. Some people choose a veterinarian based on her proximity, availability, or fees. However, intangibles such as the vet's personality and knowledge are also important to consider. You can find information about local veterinarians through veterinary association listings. For example, the Association of Exotic Mammal Veterinarians Web site (www.aemv.org) contains a national

listing of members that treat ferrets and other small mammals.

Once you draw up a list of possibilities, call all the clinics and ask questions about their hours of operation, emergency coverage, prices, and the veterinarian's experience. The clinic with the lowest fees or the clinic closest to your home might not be the best one. Try to find one that can provide quality care but that also seems to have fair prices and is within a reasonable driving distance. Remember, in an emergency, the great vet forty minutes away might not seem like such a good choice.

When you narrow down the choices, plan a visit to each hospital

A good place to start when looking for a veterinarian to care for your ferret is the Web site of the Association of Exotic Mammal Veterinarians (AEMV). The site, at www.aemv.org, includes a database of veterinarians who are trained to care for small pets.

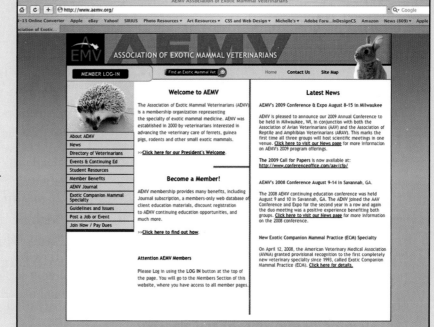

and ask to meet the veterinarian. Observe how the staff treats patients and clients, and be alert to the veterinarian's manner. Individual personalities may vary, but the veterinarian should always be open, honest, and willing to answer your questions. This is the time to ask for a hospital tour, as well as to ask questions about the veterinarian's experience. Most veterinarians are happy to talk with owners. If a veterinarian or the clinic staff seems reluctant to answer questions, or if the facility does not have an open door policy or will not make a trial appointment for you, this might be how they deal with owners when their pets are sick. When a veterinarian is open and willing to take time to explain things to you, that is a definite plus.

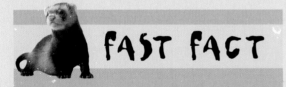

FAST FACT

A good veterinary hospital should have at least one certified veterinary technician, if not more. Veterinary technicians are highly trained clinic staff who are licensed by the state and have at least two years of college education in animal handling and medicine. A technician can answer questions when the doctor is not available, and is an important part of a ferret's health care team.

Some veterinarians devote their practice exclusively to treating exotic animals, like ferrets, birds, and snakes, and may even have advanced training in this area. Exotic animal clinics are a great place to take a ferret, but they may not be located close by. They can also be highly in demand, so make sure they are taking new patients.

Another option is a veterinarian in general practice who also treats ferrets. Most towns have at least one or two vets like this. While these doctors may not have the breadth of experience that an exotic veterinarian does, they can handle most issues involving ferrets, particularly if they are enthusiastic and are willing to continually educate themselves on ferrets and their health. They are also typically happy to refer any cases that might be beyond the scope of their knowledge and experience. Ask these veterinarians if they have a referral network for difficult cases and how willing they are to use it.

Ask all veterinarians you are considering how long they have been treating ferrets, how many ferrets they see, and what kind of continuing education programs they attend on ferret health. Also ask about the clinic's staff and their individual training. Finally, let impressions about the clinic itself, the staff, and other issues, such as hours of operation and distance from home, complete the picture.

THE VETERINARY EXAM

Few tools are as important to an animal's health as a thorough exam by a knowledgeable veterinarian. When a veterinarian examines a pet, he is looking at both the entire animal and the individual systems. Many owners question if annual exams are necessary, feeling that all an animal really needs is vaccinations. In reality, the exam is the single most powerful tool a veterinarian has to see if an animal is sick or healthy.

Before the exam begins, either the veterinarian or his technician will ask a list of questions about the ferret's appetite, bathroom habits, and other concerns. These questions are part of the exam and highlight any problems the veterinarian might expect to find.

Once the exam is underway, note how the doctor handles the ferret. His attitude should be calm and reassuring. He will examine the ferret's eyes, teeth, and ears, then proceed down the ferret's body, palpating the abdomen and limbs, and listening to the heart and lungs. The doctor will often observe the ferret interacting in the environment and

REACTIONS TO VACCINES

Vaccinations are efficient and safe ways to prevent disease, but some animals do have reactions to vaccines. While most vaccine reactions are thought to occur with distemper vaccines, reaction to rabies vaccination has also been recorded. Most veterinarians recommend that ferret owners stay at the clinic for about thirty minutes after a vaccine is administered, in case the ferret has a reaction. Signs of a reaction include vomiting, bloody diarrhea, fever, drooling, and difficulty breathing. If a reaction occurs, the veterinarian will give the ferret a shot to stop the reaction and may administer other emergency treatment. The ferret will then need to be monitored for the next few days and treated with medication as necessary, until the reaction abates.

Most ferrets that have a reaction will need to be pretreated with medicine before future vaccinations or not vaccinated from that time on. The ferret's veterinarian will discuss these options and come up with the best plan for the individual ferret. Keep in mind that the protection vaccines offer far outweighs the risk of possible reaction.

will also take the animal's tempera-ture and heart rate. Some ferrets are easy to handle. Others might wiggle and need a bit of restraint. Don't be surprised if the veterinary technician scruffs the ferret to make parts of the exam go more smoothly. Most ferrets relax in this posture, and it is not painful to them.

After the exam, the doctor will go over all the findings, both normal and abnormal. A normal animal should have bright, clear eyes, clean white teeth, and a thick, slightly greasy coat. The skin and body should be free of lumps and bumps, and the heart and lungs free of abnormal sounds. The ferret should be curious and alert and move with-out stiffness or weakness.

Abnormalities, such as heart mur-murs, growths, or dental disease, might indicate the need for further treatment or testing.

Laboratory samples are often taken at this time, including fecal and blood samples. Ferrets may require sedation to have blood drawn, but typically this is very brief, and they recover almost immediately. Additional testing, such as x-rays, may be performed. Lab tests are rou-tinely run on ferrets, even if they aren't sick, to help detect various diseases early on. The doctor should also explain the purpose of any tests she runs, what she is looking for, and what the results mean.

VACCINATIONS

Most veterinarians practice preven-tative care, including parasite con-trol, dental care, and vaccinations. Unlike dogs and cats, ferrets don't require a large number of vaccines: Only rabies and canine distemper vaccines are currently approved for ferrets. Both vaccinations are important to a ferret's health, but rabies vaccination is also required by law.

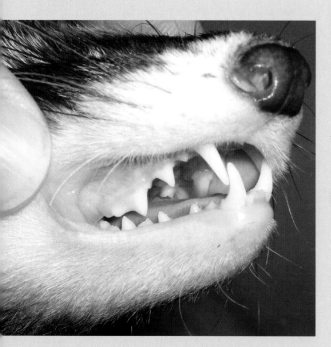

Your ferret's first veterinary exam is an important one. Your vet will check your ferret's teeth, fur, and skin, and may draw blood samples as well.

Canine distemper is a viral disease of dogs to which ferrets are highly susceptible. Distemper is fatal in unvaccinated ferrets, so you must build up your ferret's immunity to it. While several vaccines for canine distemper exist, there are only two that are approved for ferrets—Fervac-D and Purevax. These vaccines are specially modified for ferrets. Other distemper vaccines should not be used for ferrets, because they can actually bring on the disease.

Rabies is a virus that affects mammals. It spreads through bites or scratches from infected animals and is fatal in unvaccinated animals. Without immediate treatment, rabies is also fatal in humans. Vaccination of pet animals is your responsibility, and it provides both protection and peace of mind. Rabies has decreased drastically in the United States in the past forty years, but it is still a major cause of human and animal deaths worldwide. For ferrets, once-a-year vaccination is required by law. Imrab 3 is the only rabies vaccine currently approved for use with ferrets.

Kits are vaccinated for distemper several times, at eight, eleven, and fourteen weeks, then yearly as adults. Multiple vaccines are necessary for the kit to have adequate protection. Rabies vaccination is done at around fourteen weeks and then repeated annually.

PARASITE CONTROL

Another important aspect of ferret health care is parasite control. Ferrets are susceptible to the same parasites as cats and dogs, including heartworms, fleas, ear mites, and intestinal worms.

HEARTWORMS AND INTESTINAL WORMS: Simple blood tests are run to check for heartworms, which are common in dogs and are now being seen in cats and ferrets. While the incidence of heartworms in ferrets is unknown, detection is on the rise. Heartworms are spread from infected animals by mosquito bites. Immature forms of the worm get into the ferret's blood and eventually develop into adult worms in the heart. These worms can cause heart failure and even death. Symptoms of

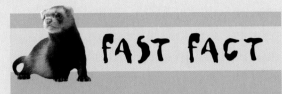

FAST FACT

Rabies is often treated in a very cavalier manner by pet owners, since it is so well controlled in the United States. However, it is a very serious matter. Unvaccinated ferrets that bite people should be quarantined; sometimes they may even be sacrificed for rabies testing.

heartworms include coughing, decreased activity, and problems breathing.

In areas where heartworms are common, all ferrets should be on a veterinarian-prescribed, monthly heartworm preventative. Treatment of heartworm disease is possible, but is very dangerous and sometimes even deadly. Prevention is key to keeping your ferret safe.

Intestinal worms are occasionally found in ferrets. A positive stool sample is a sign that a ferret has worms and should be treated with the appropriate medication. Ferrets can get worms outside, through litter boxes, or by consuming uncooked food. To prevent a ferret from getting worms, avoid exposing it to other animals and feed it commercial ferret food.

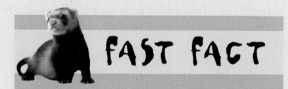

FAST FACT

In warm climates, heartworms are present year-round. The Southeast, including southern Texas and the Mississippi Valley, has more cases of heartworm per year than any other part of the country. A mosquito carrying heartworms can range for more than two miles, and indoor pets, such as ferrets, are just as susceptible as pets kept outdoors.

EAR MITES: Ear mites are common in ferrets, particularly young ferrets or ferrets that live with cats or dogs. Mites are contagious between animals and can be hard to control. A sign of ear mites is a thick, black, crusty discharge in the ears that is different from normal ear wax. Treatment consists of ear drops or an injection. To prevent ear mites, make sure new animals in a house are healthy, keep other animals (particularly cats) inside, and if one of your animals has ear mites, treat all the animals in your home, not just the infected ones.

SKIN MITES: The disease caused by skin mites, called sarcoptic mange or scabies, can be spread to ferrets even without direct contact between a ferret and an infected animal. Seek medical attention for a ferret that scratches constantly, has trouble walking, or has patchy fur. Other signs of skin mite infection include reddened, swollen feet; small, red pustules; and yellowish crust on the skin. Veterinarians typically prescribe topical ivermectin to treat ferrets with skin mites. Keep an eye out for symptoms and take the same preventative measures as with ear mites. As with ear mite infection, treat all your pets if one of them has skin mites. If untreated, skin mites cause fur loss and severe skin problems, and are sometimes deadly.

FLEAS: The most common parasite ferret owners deal with is the flea. Fleas are small, quick, blood-sucking insects, which are a major pest. Even indoor ferrets can get fleas, and ferrets that live with dogs and cats are particularly susceptible. Fleas are typically seen as small, black, fast-moving bugs on the belly or around the tail and head. They will often leave black specks in the ferret's fur; these specks are actually flea feces and are made up of dried blood. Fleas cause itchiness and can cause hair loss and other health problems. When fleas are found on a ferret, it means they are also present in the environment.

Flea baths or powders that just kill fleas that are on an animal for a short time are usually ineffective in

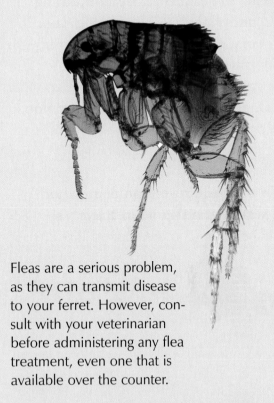

Fleas are a serious problem, as they can transmit disease to your ferret. However, consult with your veterinarian before administering any flea treatment, even one that is available over the counter.

controlling a flea problem. The best way to prevent fleas is to use a veterinarian-prescribed topical medication on the ferret and on all other pets in a household. While not approved for this use, products for cats, such as Frontline, Advantage, and Program, can be used under a veterinarian's direction. Never use any products for dogs or any over-the-counter cat products on a ferret without asking a veterinarian first. Flea products containing pyrethrins, which are safe for kittens, can be used for ferrets, but most over-the-counter products are

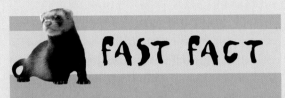

FAST FACT

Adult fleas—what most people see—actually only represent about 10 percent of all fleas in the environment; the other 90 percent are in one of the other stages of development—egg, larva, or pupa. A female flea can lay up to 2000 eggs in her lifetime.

toxic, especially those containing organophosphates or dichlorvos. It is very easy to overdose a ferret, even with safe products like pyrethrins, so be cautious. Always ask a veterinarian first if what you plan to use is safe.

THE SICK FERRET

Of course, prevention is only part of a veterinarian's role in a ferret's health. Most people recognize that a veterinarian's most important job is treating sick or injured animals. When a ferret is sick, hours can count, so learning how to detect the early signs of illness can help make sure your ferret is treated as soon as possible. A ferret that has been sick for days and is weak and dehydrated may be beyond help, especially in the case of serious illness.

WHEN YOUR FERRET REFUSES TO EAT

One of the most common problems encountered with a sick or injured ferret is decreased appetite. Many ferrets that are sick will refuse to eat at all. While refusal to eat is a symptom of many diseases, it actually becomes a problem in and of itself if it goes on for too long. Recovering from any illness is made difficult as a result of poor nutrition, and special measures may become necessary to boost your ferret's appetite.

Many ferret experts and veterinarians have recipes for a concoction called "duck soup." Duck soup doesn't really contain duck; it is usually a mixture of meat, ferret food, and supplements. Recipes are available all over the Internet and vary widely. Some are not very nutritious at all, so make sure that any recipe you follow comes from a reputable source. The mixture is a bit like a "meat shake" and is fed through a syringe. While some ferrets eat the mixture willingly, there is concern among many veterinarians about force feeding a sick animal any sort of liquid diet. Ferrets will sometimes fight this mixture, and there is a risk they can choke on or aspirate the soup into their airway, particularly in inexperienced hands. Aspirating liquids of any kind can lead to pneumonia, which will worsen problems.

Another option that has been tried and true throughout the years is chicken baby food. Many people use chicken baby food as a treat for ferrets normally, and even very sick ferrets will often eat it. It is calorie-dense and high in protein, and can be easily fed on a spoon. Veterinary offices also carry calorie-rich recovery diets for dogs and cats that are a similar consistency to baby food and that can be fed to sick ferrets in combination with vitamin and calorie supplements, such as Nutrical.

The first things to note on a daily basis are your ferret's attitude and appetite. You know your ferret best, and if your ferret skips a meal and seems unusually quiet, this can signal that something is wrong. When a ferret is sick, call the vet as soon as possible. Hair loss, decreased appetite, increased water consumption, and general poor attitude—especially in an older ferret—are all signs that the ferret needs to visit the veterinarian. Diarrhea, vomiting, coughing, sneezing, and a runny noise are also signs of illness, as are abnormally pale or yellow skin, obvious swellings on the body, or anything else that just doesn't seem normal.

In general, if symptoms such as soft stool, coughing or sneezing, lack of appetite, or mild lethargy have gone on for more than twenty-four hours, it is always wise to call your veterinarian. If these symptoms are accompanied by pain, weakness, severe lethargy, difficulty breathing, profuse vomiting or diarrhea, or the inability to move, or if the ferret has been observed eating something dangerous or toxic, the situation qualifies as an emergency and the ferret needs to be seen immediately, even in the middle of the night.

After a physical exam, a veterinarian may recommend blood tests, x-rays, as well as emergency medical treatment. Blood tests and x-rays check for the presence of disease and also help pinpoint the possible cause of an animal's illness.

COMMON HEALTH PROBLEMS

The thought of a beloved pet being ill is enough to make most pet owners worry, but when a pet actually becomes ill, things can be overwhelming. Blood results, medicines, and treatments can all form a big, mixed-up jumble, and it is sometimes hard to figure out what is going on. Having general knowledge of the problems a ferret may encounter can help you ask appropriate questions and give you some peace of mind during a nerve-wracking time.

GASTROINTESTINAL PROBLEMS: Stomach and intestinal problems make up a good percentage of ferret emergency visits, and viruses, blockages, and bacterial infections are all possible causes. Take a ferret with vomiting or diarrhea to the veterinarian as soon as possible, particularly if you suspect that the cause is a foreign body. A foreign body is an object a ferret eats that then becomes stuck in the ferret's stomach or intestines. Foreign bodies are extremely common, especially among kits. Almost anything can become a

If your ferret seems sick or is acting abnormally, you'll need to hand-feed him about every four hours to make sure that he's getting proper nutrition. Also, make sure that your ferret is drinking, because ferrets can become dehydrated easily when they are not feeling well. If necessary, you may have to bottle-feed your ailing pet.

foreign body including pieces of foam, rubber, strings, wires, and indigestible pieces of food, such as chunks of apple. Older ferrets will sometimes develop foreign bodies from hairballs. The best ways to prevent your ferret from ingesting a foreign body are good ferret-proofing and hairball control.

A ferret with a foreign body is a medical emergency. The ferret may suffer from diarrhea, weakness, and stomach pain, as well as signs of nausea, including drooling and pawing at its mouth. Foreign bodies can often be detected by feeling the stomach or

by x-rays, and the treatment is usually surgery to remove the object. Success is often based on how quickly the foreign body can be removed. Some foreign bodies can cause damage to the stomach or intestines, and, in these cases, the animal's recovery is much less certain.

Other gastrointestinal diseases seen in the ferret include ulcers, inflammatory bowel disease, bacterial disease, and viruses. These have various symptoms and treatments, but most cause diarrhea, with or without blood, loss of appetite, and weight loss. Vomiting is unusual, except in the case of ulcers. Inflammatory bowel disease is often related to a food allergy, and one virus, Epizootic Catarrhal Enteritis, is characterized by bright green stools that give it the nickname "green slime disease." Treatment consists of medications specific to the illness and fluids, for dehydration, when needed. All these conditions respond best to treatment when it is started early. Time wasted often puts a ferret at risk.

NON-DIGESTIVE ILLNESSES: A wide range of illnesses can affect ferrets, including viruses, parasites, heart problems, and tumors. Viral diseases, such as distemper, rabies, Aleutian disease, and respiratory infections, have varying symptoms and effects. Distemper causes severe respiratory problems and, in advanced cases, signs such as seizures and tremors. Rabies causes paralysis, confusion, fever, and abnormal behavior. Rabies is communicable to people, and while both distemper and rabies are fatal in ferrets, they are also preventable through vaccination. Aleutian disease is a highly contagious, wasting disease of ferrets that has no treatment. Ferrets can be carriers of this disease for years before they develop symptoms.

Ferrets are particularly susceptible to respiratory infections, including human influenza and colds. Human colds can make a ferret very ill and even lead to pneumonia, so be sure to keep ferrets away from sick people and use strict hygienic practices when handling them.

Heartworms, intestinal worms, fleas, ear mites, and skin mites can all cause disease but are easily prevented with proper care (see "Parasite Control," earlier in this chapter). Other conditions, such as bladder stones, are preventable with proper diet. Bladder stones can cause painful urination or urinary blockage and are usually treated surgically.

Heart problems and tumors are usually diagnosed during a physical exam. Heart conditions are often treated with medication, whereas the treatment of tumors depends on their type and location. Some common tumors are benign, including a type of skin tumor called a mast cell tumor. These tumors almost always respond well to surgery, provided the tumor is detected early. Other, more serious, tumors can affect the lymph nodes, intestines, and other organs and may be more difficult to treat.

HORMONAL DISEASE

The final group of illnesses that affects ferrets is also the most common. Older ferrets are at high risk of developing hormone-related illnesses, especially adrenal disease and insulinoma. A third disease, hyper-estrogenism, affects unspayed jills.

ADRENAL GLAND DISEASE: Adrenal gland disease typically occurs in older ferrets, has a slow course, and is the most common illness of ferrets in the United States. In recent years, a link has been suspected between early spaying and neutering of ferrets and adrenal problems later in life, although the actual cause is not known. The adrenal glands are tiny organs in the body with a big job. They produce many of the hormones and chemicals that help the body run properly. Adrenal gland disease is a type of cancer. When the cancerous adrenal glands become enlarged, they begin to produce too much hormone. High hormone levels lead to disease and can cause life-threatening complications.

The first symptom of adrenal gland disease is symmetrical hair loss on both sides of the body that begins at the rear and eventually works towards the head. As the condition worsens, other symptoms include itchy skin, a potbelly, muscle weakness and loss of muscle tone, and, in females, enlargement of the vulva.

Eventually, serious problems can occur, including anemia and bleeding disorders from the hormone's effects on the bone marrow and, in males, an enlarged prostate, which can cause problems urinating. Males can also become more aggressive.

Veterinarians diagnose adrenal gland disease by a combination of exam findings, ultrasound, and blood work. There are two treatments: surgery to remove the cancerous glands or medication to control the hormone levels. Surgery may be highly effective, but is often difficult, due to the adrenal gland's location. Another potential complication comes from anesthesia, which is always risky in the ferret. Most ferrets will survive for several years after surgery, even if the tumor is not completely removed. The second treatment is Lupron, a once-monthly injection. Lupron (a drug used in the treatment of human prostate cancer) controls hormone levels, but can be very expensive.

INSULINOMA: A second hormonal condition, insulinoma, is also very common in older ferrets. Insulinoma consists of multiple tumors in the pancreas, the organ that produces insulin and regulates blood sugar. The tumors generate large amounts of insulin, which brings down a ferret's blood sugar. Low blood sugar causes sluggishness and, at extremely low levels, can lead to seizures, coma, and death. The disease has a slow onset, and, at first, a ferret may simply lose weight and seem a bit more tired than usual. As the disease progresses, the ferret can suffer from symptoms such as drooling, tremors, and severe lethargy, and may even collapse.

Insulinoma is diagnosed by blood tests and can be confirmed by a biopsy. There are two treatments—medication and surgery—but neither offers a complete cure. Surgery removes visible nodules and decreases the size of large tumors, but the nodules can be extremely tiny, and it is impossible to remove them all. Medication is given to patients after surgery or as treatment by itself. A steroid called Prednisone, which helps boost blood sugar, is used either alone or with Diazoxide, a medicine that decreases the effects of insulin. The animal is also fed small meals consisting of high amounts of protein and fat throughout the day, with all sugars banned from the diet. The prognosis for insulinoma is improved if it is detected and treated early. The longer a ferret is ill before being treated, the poorer its response. On average, ferrets live about a year to a year and a half after diagnosis.

HYPERESTROGENISM: One final hormonal condition, hyperestrogenism, is relatively rare, due to the high percentage of spayed female ferrets, but can be quite serious. Unspayed female ferrets can develop the disease at any time after they come into heat, most commonly between one and two years. Once they come into heat, female ferrets stay in heat until they breed. If intact females do not become pregnant, after one or two months the high levels of the hormone estrogen begin to affect their body. Symptoms of the disease are similar to those of adrenal gland disease, with hair loss and an enlarged vulva. As the disease worsens, the bone marrow will decrease production of blood cells because of the high amounts of estrogen. This leads to anemia, which can be life-threatening.

The treatment of hyperestrogenism is spaying. Ferrets with low cell levels need a hormone injection to bring them out of their heat before surgery is performed. Once the ferret's anemia improves, the ferret is spayed. Very sick animals will also need to be hospitalized for further treatment.

CHAPTER SEVEN

Enjoying Your Ferret

Ferrets live to play. It is the only pressing matter on their agenda beyond eating and sleeping. In fact, if it wasn't a misnomer, you could almost call having a good time their job. They are natural clowns and entertainers and never fail to bring joy and laughter to a home. Of course, they tend to get into trouble and make a bit of a mess along the way. To some people, ferrets probably sound like a lot of work. Ferrets are time-consuming, occasionally expensive, and they need a lot of looking after. That said, however, it's important to remember that the reason most people get a ferret is because they are simply so much fun.

Your funny little ferret will play with just about anything he can get his paws on.

FUN AND GAMES

Entertaining ferrets isn't hard. Put ferrets in an empty room and they'll find something to occupy themselves. That's not too much fun though, particularly when there are so many games and diversions to entertain them. A ferret's favorite plaything is, and always should be, its owner. No amount of expensive

Peek a boo! Your ferret will find the funniest hiding places throughout your home.

FAST FACT

Some of the best ferret toys can be found at home—and on a budget. Cardboard box mazes, pairs of rolled-up socks, and ping-pong balls are all ferret favorites. A beloved, if messy, plaything is a "sandbox," a plastic pan or cardboard box filled with potting soil or sand. Ferrets will play for hours digging and burrowing, then owners can spend hours cleaning up the mess.

toys set in a cage can take the place of daily playtime and interaction with a ferret's favorite humans.

Ferrets will play with just about anything. They have a fine time playing with each other or with their human friends, but in the absence of others, they can still have a rollicking good time. Ferrets tend to gallop through life with all four feet. They jump, run, tumble, and burrow. When really happy and playful, ferrets execute a characteristic movement referred to as the "ferret war dance." This involves the ferret bouncing around on all four feet, back arched, and making a happy chattering noise that most people call "dooking." Some people at first think their ferret has gone a bit crazy, but dooking is

When your ferret arches his back, bristles his fur, and hisses, it's a sign that he's unhappy or angry. Avoid a hissing ferret, as they are likely to bite. Wait until he has calmed down before you try to hold him.

actually a sign that the ferret is having a grand time.

Fancy toys for ferrets abound in pet stores, but great fun can be had with almost anything, as long as it is safe. Ferrets love to play with balls, cat toys, tubes, and tunnels to crawl through, but paper bags, cardboard boxes, and even pillowcases can provide hours of enjoyment. They also have a blast attacking human toes and feet, and most owners quickly learn to keep shoes on when their ferret is in attack mode.

When choosing toys, remember that safety comes first. Avoid any toys with small parts or rubber or foam that could be easily chewed off and swallowed.

Games can be many and varied, but some ferret favorites include tug-of-war, chase, and wrestling. All that is required for these are simple materials, such as a towel, a cat feather toy, and of course, a willing human playmate. Most ferrets will eagerly grab onto the edge of a towel and engage in a pulling fight. They also love to be dragged around the room with their owner pulling one end of the towel and them resisting on the other. Often the game ends abruptly when the ferret grabs the towel and runs away to stash it in a hiding place.

Ferrets love to chase their humans around and they love to be chased. They will also go wild with a ball or some feathers on a string. Laser pointers are also favorite toys, letting them stalk, tumble, and run as they chase the little red dot.

These forms of play mimic a ferret's natural behavior in the wild. Ferrets play together by chasing each other and engaging in mock combat. Both are ways to improve their hunting and chasing abilities, all while having fun. When coming up with games to play, just think about what ferrets naturally do. They'll usually do the rest.

TRAVELING WITH AND WITHOUT YOUR FERRET

At some point, most ferret owners will have to leave town. In some cases, bringing the pet ferret along is part of the fun, particularly if a visit to family is on the agenda. Often, however, the ferret needs to stay behind. When this happens, there are several ferret-care options available.

WHEN THE FERRET STAYS HOME: The best person to care for a pet ferret is someone the ferret already knows and likes. Friends, close neighbors, and family members who are willing to help out can be a lifesaver. There are several benefits to having a familiar pet sitter—including the added security of knowing that your ferret will be safe and comfortable in its own home. Friends and family members are trustworthy and will often watch a pet as a favor, as opposed to having to hire a paid sitter. On the downside, sometimes it can be hard to find someone willing to commit to watching a ferret, particularly for a long time. One other drawback is that because ferrets require daily playtime, a pet sitter

Try using the PetSit.com Web site to help you find a suitable ferret sitter.

might need to visit for several hours a day or even keep the ferret in her own home.

When a friend or family member is unavailable, a professional pet sitter is another option. Because ferrets require so much time and work, a pet sitter can be somewhat expensive, depending on what exactly she is required to do. Many pet sitters won't sit for ferrets or other small animals, but if they do, make sure they are experienced, licensed and bonded. Pet sitters do exactly what the name says—they care for pets. They aren't employed to water plants or collect mail, although some might do this as a favor. Pet sitters are paid professionals who visit the house daily or, in some cases, actually spend the night. Professional pet sitting isn't cheap (typically in the range of $15–$30 per visit, depending on how many ferrets you have and what services you request), but it is a good value considering the peace of mind that comes with knowing your pet is well cared for. The best way to find pet sitters is by asking friends or the ferret's veterinarian for recommendations. Most vets are familiar with local sitters and their reputations. Web sites, such as the site of Pet Sitters International (www.petsit.com), are also a great place to look.

Another option is boarding at a kennel or an animal hospital. The cost of boarding will usually be less than a pet sitter, but there are drawbacks to this option. Unless a ferret is boarded at a very fancy resort kennel where playtime options are available, most ferrets will spend the majority of the time in their cage. This can be stressful, as can being surrounded by a large number of unfamiliar animals and people. Stress can lead to illness, particularly considering that the ferret may be exposed to viruses and other diseases during its time at the kennel. Another downside is that most boarding facilities are not equipped for ferrets, if they even provide service for ferrets at all. At the minimum, they will probably ask an owner to bring the ferret's cage along, as well as the ferret's food and dishes. In most cases, boarding should be considered the last resort, unless there is an exceptional kennel nearby.

WHEN THE FERRET COMES ALONG: Particularly for long trips or visits to family, a final possibility is to bring your pet ferret along. Ferrets are fairly cheerful and adaptable, as long as they have familiar people and things around them, so bringing your ferrets with you can be considered as

Make air travel go as smoothly as possible by buying the appropriate-sized carrier. When ferrets are permitted to travel in the cabin, airlines typically specify that the approved carrier be soft-sided and a particular size.

INTERNATIONAL TRAVEL AND YOUR FERRET

When traveling to other countries with your ferret, you must abide by international laws and regulations. Taking your ferret within the United States and Canada to regions where ferrets are not restricted is fairly simple: you must have a health certificate from a USDA-accredited veterinarian and proof of rabies vaccination. When traveling internationally, however, the health certificate must be signed by a representative of the USDA as well, typically within ten days of travel. Further paperwork may be required by the country the ferret is traveling to. Some countries require simple documentation, but many, including parts of Europe, Australia, and Asia, have much more stringent requirements.

European countries require an additional certificate signed by a veterinarian and stating that flea and tick medication has been applied within the last month. Many countries also require proof of yearly rabies vaccination, even if the vaccine is licensed for longer periods.

Nations that quarantine for rabies, including the United Kingdom and the Cayman Islands, require either a long, expensive quarantine (as long as six months) or, alternatively, special blood tests for rabies levels and a six-month waiting period prior to entering the country. Most countries require ferrets to have permanent identification, such as a microchip, and some nations ban the importation of ferrets entirely.

So, except in cases of a long-term move, traveling internationally with your ferret should probably be avoided.

long as they are welcome at their destination. For some people, bringing their fuzzy along seems like a perfect solution, but it does have drawbacks, especially when air travel is involved.

When traveling with a ferret, keep in mind that the ferret isn't the only thing that's traveling. Your fuzzy will need a cage, litter box, food and water, and pretty much everything it needs at home. With car trips this is more manageable, but flying is often quite difficult for this reason. Many airlines won't even allow ferrets on board a plane, and very few will allow them to accompany their owner inside the cabin. Before making travel plans by air, check airline policy to see if your carrier accommodates ferrets.

Wherever the destination or the mode of transportation, remember to ferret-proof the new environment, as well as to be vigilant for other pets, escape routes, and hidden dangers.

When traveling by car, make sure never to leave a ferret unattended. Just a few minutes in a locked car can be dangerous, even at moderate temperatures. Ferrets cannot sweat and are extremely sensitive to increases in temperature. Even with the windows open they can quickly develop heatstroke and die. Taking pet ferrets on a trip could be devastating if they end up lost or harmed in any way.

FUN ACTIVITIES FOR OWNERS AND FERRETS

Ferret enthusiasts are everywhere. A good way to meet them and possibly to make some new friends is by joining a local ferret association. Most areas have some sort of loosely organized group of ferret fanciers. One way to find them is by looking on the Internet or asking at veterinary offices or pet stores if there are any groups in the area. These groups organize shows, symposiums, and other events that are often both educational and entertaining.

Symposiums are national ferret events that combine shows, lectures, and exhibits. Several different organizations host symposiums, usually on an annual basis. Symposiums, which are a little like conventions, are a good place for owners to learn more about ferrets, to buy fun toys or gadgets, and, of course, to show off their fuzzies.

FERRETS ON THE JOB

Ferrets can be more than just natural mischief makers that sleep a lot. Some ferrets actually work for a living.

Over the years, electricians and engineers have used ferrets to help lay cables and wires in tight spaces. Ferrets helped lay guide wires for the Boeing Company and also for British Columbia Telephone. While these ferrets were ideal for fitting into the tight spaces, engineers sometimes encountered problems when the ferrets would rather sleep and play in the tubes than finish their work.

Ferrets are also stars of the big and small screen. Ferrets have appeared in many major motion pictures and often steal the show from their human costars. Ferrets have appeared in the movies *Kindergarten Cop, Starship Troopers, Along Came Polly*, and many others. With their natural star quality and winning expressions, it is easy to see how the ferret has become a highly sought-after animal actor.

A typical ferret show, like dog or cat shows, lets ferrets compete for titles in different categories, including those for kits and adults, as well as those by color, breeding status, and sometimes whimsical categories, such as Best Spirit or Most Lovable.

Ferret shows are great fun and are a good way for owners to bond with their ferrets as well as to meet other ferret lovers. All ferrets participating in shows are required to be up-to-date on vaccinations and, in some cases, tested for contagious diseases.

Showing your ferret is a wonderful way to socialize your pet with other ferrets, and also a great way for you to meet other ferret enthusiasts.

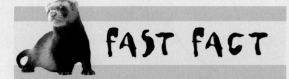

FAST FACT

The American Ferret Association Web site (www.ferret.org) lists shows and national symposiums, and is a great place to find local ferret activities and groups. Show organizers often work with ferret rescue leagues as well, which can be fun and fulfilling places to volunteer.

TO BREED OR NOT TO BREED

Breeding ferrets is very difficult. It can be hard to find ferrets that are appropriate parents for breeding, and a great deal of work is required to properly socialize young ferrets so they become good pets. Also, there are already large numbers of ferrets in shelters and rescue organizations that are in need of good homes; breeding more only compounds this problem. Therefore, a ferret owner should not consider breeding until she has owned ferrets for a long time and has become extremely knowledgeable about their care. You should attend ferret association meetings and symposiums, and talk with breeders and other ferret experts before even thinking about breeding as an option.

Becoming a ferret breeder involves a major commitment of both time and space. This is not something that a novice ferret owner should consider. If you are considering breeding ferrets, talk to established breeders. They will be able to give you a sense of the difficulties and rewards of this job.

Breeders must have a hob readily available for the moment when a jill comes into heat. Remember, if jills are not bred, they will continue to cycle and eventually become ill from anemia (see "Hyperestrogenism" in Chapter 6). This usually means having an intact hob right on the premises. Intact males are smelly and oily, and most people who keep ferrets in their home would find them difficult to live with. Hobs can also be aggressive when they're in season, especially with the female.

Jills will need to be spayed after having given birth, unless the breeder plans on having them give birth to another litter in the future. Once they have successfully bred, gestation lasts around forty-two days. The

An important part of breeding and raising baby ferrets is socializing them to humans and beginning their training.

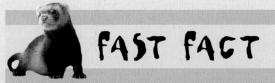

female will give birth to an average of eight kits, but can have as many as eighteen at a time.

At birth, baby ferrets are completely bald, blind, and very small, but grow quickly, reaching weaning age at about six to eight weeks. At around three weeks, it is extremely important to begin socializing baby ferrets with humans. This is a lengthy and time-consuming process, particularly with a large litter. It is essential, however, in order to produce ferrets that will fit in properly with their human family and not have behavior problems.

All in all, most breeders, veterinarians, and experts advise against breeding ferrets for anyone who does not have extensive experience and resources. Newborn ferrets are adorable, but they are also a lot of work.

CHAPTER EIGHT

Your Aging Ferret

When you purchase a young ferret, the time when he will reach old age may seem like it is very far away. In reality, though, ferrets typically live for only five to eight years and are considered senior citizens starting around the age of four. Some ferrets live as long as eleven or twelve, but, unfortunately, this is the exception rather than the rule.

Older ferrets may slow down a little. While still inquisitive and playful, they sleep a bit more and move a bit more slowly. They may not jump as high or climb as far, and may be content with more snuggle time than playtime, especially

You can expect to spend five to eight years enjoying your ferret's company.

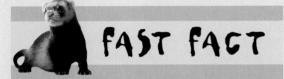

if they are ill or very advanced in age.

Four years old is considered the starting point of old age because that is the time when health problems, such as adrenal disease and insulinoma, are usually first observed. Many ferrets don't develop health problems until even later, but it is important to closely observe ferrets of all ages for signs of illness or behavioral changes that could signal health problems.

Most veterinarians recommend that older ferrets receive wellness checkups every six months. These checkups include a thorough physical exam and possibly blood tests or x-rays. In between visits, close monitoring at home of the ferret's body condition is essential. Hair loss, weight loss, or other abnormalities are signs that an extra trip to the veterinarian is needed.

SPECIAL CONCERNS

Other than allowing for a general slowing down, a senior ferret doesn't need to be treated much differently than a younger ferret. After all, old age itself isn't a disease! Still, it's a good idea to consider switching an older ferret onto a specially formulated food for seniors. These diets are typically lower in fat and are more appropriate for a less active animal. Most companies that produce ferret food also have a senior variety, and you should buy the senior food made by the same manufacturer. When making a switch, always mix the old and new foods together over several days to avoid diarrhea and to keep the ferret from turning up its nose at a new food.

No matter what food a ferret eats, it's always important to closely monitor its appetite. Increased or

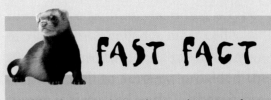

As your ferret ages, he won't be as energetic as he once was. He'll still enjoy time spent playing with you, but you may find that he appreciates snuggling more than he did when he was younger.

decreased appetite is often the first sign of illness. Ferrets tend to have more health problems as they age, so it is very important to keep a close eye on them.

The most common illnesses a senior ferret is prone to are adrenal disease, insulinoma, and other types of cancer (see Chapter 6). As previously discussed, these diseases can often be treated, at least for a time, especially if they are caught early.

One important issue with older ferrets is quality of life. Quality of life refers to the health, general comfort, and freedom from pain of an individual animal. Most ferrets will eventually experience a decline in their quality of life that is not responsive to medical treatment.

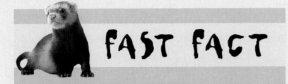

FAST FACT

Once ferrets start having problems climbing, rearrange their environment to make things easier for them. Cage ramps and hammocks may have to go, and ferrets may take up permanent residence on their cage floor. Lowering the sides of litter boxes, for ease of entry and exit, is also a good idea.

Unfortunately, as with all pets, there comes a time when a decision has to be made.

SAYING GOOD-BYE

When a new ferret arrives, the eventual loss of a beloved friend is something that seems like it could never happen. This section might not apply right now, but its purpose is to address how to respond when the time comes to say good-bye and to serve as a valuable resource to aid the decision and to help with the grieving process.

Most veterinarians say that when it's time to say good-bye you will know, and this is very much the truth. You know your ferret better than anyone and you certainly know when it is no longer getting enjoyment from its days. The decision to say good-bye is a difficult one, and many factors come into play at that time. Factors to consider are the ferret's overall health, whether the ferret is in pain, how often the ferret is capable of doing the things that it used to enjoy, and how the ferret's illness or disease is affecting the bond between ferret and owner.

In rare cases, a ferret will pass away on its own. In this case, the decision is taken away from the owners and they are able to move on to the grieving process. When a decision must be made, however, the ferret's veterinarian is often the best person to consult. Ask the veterinarian questions about long-term prognosis and quality of life as well as any questions about the process of euthanasia.

Most veterinarians and owners refer to euthanasia as putting an animal to sleep. In fact, the procedure is much like falling asleep and should be completely painless for the animal and as painless as possible for the owner. Many veterinarians sedate the ferret first, so it is calm and relaxed. Sometimes, an owner may not be present for the actual injection, depending on the animal's health, but typically, owners are welcome and encouraged to stay, both to say good-bye and to take comfort in how truly peaceful their pet's last moments are.

Making a decision to put a beloved pet to sleep is never easy, but often the buildup to the actual decision is more difficult than the loss itself. Many pet owners agonize over whether they are doing the right thing, only to come to a moment of peace when they realize that their friend is no longer suffering.

MOVING ON

After the loss of any pet, particularly one larger than life like a ferret, it can be difficult to move on. The house is often quieter and emptier, and things may seem a bit dull and sad. Each one of us is different in how long it takes us to mourn and in what way, but as time passes, the sad memories are replaced by all the joyful ones that were shared over the years. A new project, talking with friends, and sometimes talking with other people who have recently lost a pet all help on the road to healing.

When a beloved pet dies, many people feel that they never want to have another animal. For some this

MOURNING RITES

All of us grieve the loss of a pet in our own way. Some people grieve as strongly as they would for a human family member. Other people try to soldier on and "tough it out." Remember that a pet is part of its owners' life for many years and shares a strong bond with them. A vital step in overcoming the loss of a pet is talking about that pet with friends, veterinarians, and family members. The AVMA also keeps a list of pet loss support hotlines. These hotlines have trained staffers on hand who listen and who can help owners through a difficult time.

For some people, planning a simple memorial, such as a photo collage, or collecting the ferret's footprint for a memory album, can be helpful. Others decide to bury their pet with other family pets and have a small memorial service or to have their remains cremated and the ashes saved in an urn to either scatter or display.

However you decide to mourn the passing and celebrate the life of a beloved pet, it is the right choice. It is normal and healthy to be sad, to cry, and to feel a strong sense of loss, but also remember that, during their lives, most ferrets live fully and well, and pack each day full of exciting experiences. Remember these good times and the curious troublemaker that the ferret was during its life, and eventually these memories will be a source of comfort, not of sadness.

A memorial garden can be a good place to remember a beloved pet. Planting a tree or a flowering shrub where a pet's remains are buried can provide a lasting place to keep its memory alive. Memorial stones can be inscribed with a pet's name, or even a picture, and can be a special touch.

is true, but the majority of people come to realize over time that the love and companionship their pet provided can best live on by taking that memory and bringing it full circle, by renewing the human-animal bond in a new relationship with another pet. When and how to do this differs from person to person, but the best advice is this: You will know when you are ready to open up your heart again, just as you knew from the beginning that your ferret was right for you.

Organizations to Contact

Association of Exotic Mammal Veterinarians
P.O. Box 396
Weare, NH 03281-0396
Fax: 603-529-4980
E-mail: info@aemv.org
Web site: www.aemv.org

The American Ferret Association
PMB 255
626-C Admiral Dr.
Annapolis, MD 21401
Phone: 888-FERRET-1
Fax: 801-927-9818
E-mail: afa@ferret.org
Web site: www.ferret.org

American Heartworm Society
P.O. Box 667
Batavia, IL 60510
Fax: 630-208-8398
E-mail: info@heartwormsociety.org
Web site: www.heartwormsociety.org

American Veterinary Medical Association
1931 North Meacham Road, Suite 100
Schaumburg, IL 60173-4360
Phone: 847-925-8070
Fax: 847-925-1329
E-mail: avmainfo@avma.org
Web site: www.avma.org

American Society for the Prevention of Cruelty to Animals (ASPCA)
424 E. 92nd St
New York, NY 10128-6804
Phone: 212-876-7700
Web site: www.aspca.org

Legalize Ferrets.org
P.O. Box 3395
San Diego, CA 92163
Phone/Fax: 619-303-0645
E-mail: caferrets@legalizeferrets.org
Web site: www.legalizeferrets.org

Further Reading

Bezzant, David. *Hunting With Ferrets*. Wiltshire, UK: The Crowood Press, Ltd., 2008.

Bezzant, David. *Ferreting—A Traditional Country Pursuit*. Wiltshire, UK: The Crowood Press, Ltd., 2004.

Bucsis, Gary and Barbara Summerville. *Training Your Pet Ferret*. Hauppage, N.Y.: Barron's, 1997.

Everitt, Nicholas. *Ferrets, Rats, and Traps*. Warwickshire, UK: Read Country Books, 2005.

Land, Bobbye. *Your Outta Control Ferret*. Neptune City, N.J.: TFH Publications, 2003.

McKay, James. *Ferret Breeding: A Modern Scientific Approach*. Shrewsbury, UK: Swanhill Press, 2006.

Shefferman, Mary R. *The Wit and Wisdom of the Modern Ferrets: A Ferret's Perspective on Ferret Care*. Smithtown, N.Y.: Modern Ferret, 2000.

Wellstead, Graham. *The Ferret and Ferreting Guide*. Cincinnati, OH: F+W Publications, 2005.

Internet Resources

http://www.ferretcongress.org

The International Ferret Congress is a nonprofit, educational organization devoted to providing information on ferret care and well-being. The Congress hosts forums and symposiums around the United States where ferret lovers can discuss and learn about ferrets, their care, and related issues.

http://www.petinsurance.com/index.aspx

Veterinary Pet Insurance (VPI) is the number-one-recommended veterinary pet insurance company, with policies available for almost any kind of pet, including small mammals.

http://www.aemv.org/vetlist.cfm

The Association of Exotic Mammal Veterinarians' directory of veterinarians is searchable by state and includes a listing of what species each veterinarian treats.

http://www.petsit.com

The Pet Sitters International Web site contains a listing of certified pet sitters as well as helpful information on choosing a pet sitter. The searchable database is easy to use, and has an option to search for sitters who will take care of exotic pets.

http://www.ferretcentral.org/orgs.html

A concise listing of ferret shelters and rescue groups organized by location, Ferret Central can be a good place to find a ferret in need of a home or places to volunteer.

http://www.avma.org/careforanimals/animatedjourneys/ goodbyefriend/goodbye.asp

The American Veterinary Medical Association's grief resource site contains helpful information and guidance about the loss of a pet, including a listing of pet loss support hotlines.

Index

Numbers in **bold italics** refer to captions.

Contributors

HOLLY J. SULLIVANT, DVM, is a small-animal veterinarian and writer. She received her doctor of veterinary medicine degree from Michigan State University in 1997. After graduation, she practiced at several well-known clinics in Miami before relocating to the Tampa Bay area in 2002. She currently practices in a small, family-oriented practice and is a member of the American Veterinary Medical Association and the Association of Exotic Mammal Veterinarians. Over her years in practice, she's encountered a variety of interesting characters, including ferrets. When she's not working with animals, she is a writer of short stories and is currently completing a novel based in small town Florida. She enjoys travel and cooking, and also spends time with her family, which includes a young son and various four-legged creatures.

Senior Consulting Editor **GARY KORSGAARD, DVM,** has had a long and distinguished career in veterinary medicine. After graduating from The Ohio State University's College of Veterinary Medicine in 1963, he spent two years as a captain in the Veterinary Corps of the U.S. Army. During that time he attended the Walter Reed Army Institute of Research and became Chief of the Veterinary Division for the Sixth Army Medical Laboratory at the Presidio, San Francisco.

In 1968 Dr. Korsgaard founded the Monte Vista Veterinary Hospital in Concord, California, where he practiced for 32 years as a small animal veterinarian. He is a past president of the Contra Costa Veterinary Association, and was one of the founding members of the Contra Costa Veterinary Emergency Clinic, serving as president and board member of that hospital for nearly 30 years.

Dr. Korsgaard retired in 2000, and currently enjoys golf, hiking, international travel, and spending time with his wife Susan and their three children and four grandchildren.